THANK YOU!

Nov '22

They say it takes a village to raise a child.

I believe this.

I also believe it takes multiple sharp-eyed readers to completely proofread a book. And so, despite best efforts by three independent professionals, this book will contain typos. Perhaps even a context error or two.

Please feel free to note the page number of the passage, or snap a pic of it, and email the details to *dustan@ourmortgage-expert.com* so that future drafts can be...closer to perfection.

Thank you, please enjoy the read.

Printed in Canada

#THISISBROKERING

ISBN 978-1-5445-0447-6 *Paperback*
978-1-5445-0448-3 *Ebook*

#THISISBROKERING

DUSTAN
WOODHOUSE

PRAISE FOR BE THE BETTER BROKER

The Amazon (both .ca and .com) Reviews are in...

111 Five Star Reviews for **Volume 1** ...and counting
89 Five Star Reviews for **Volume 2** ...and counting
56 Five Star Reviews for **Volume 3** ...and counting

Please post a review of your own, and email a copy direct to *dustan@ourmortgageexpert.com* to receive a bonus chapter as a thank you.

Volume 1

INSPIRING AND CRITICALLY INFORMATIVE!

By Ron van Someren on May 23, 2017

Great read. I just honestly felt like I was sitting down and having coffee with the author as he gave some incredible insight and tips on becoming a mortgage broker. He also references some other incredible books, websites and videos that he credits that I also found extremely useful. Very good read. I am certainly going to be picking up his other books.

I AM NOW A BETTER BROKER

By Brad Lockey on March 15, 2017

Thank you Dustan for the clarity and candidness of your thought processes. I am definitely better off after reading your series.

I HAVE BEEN IN THE MORTGAGE INDUSTRY FOR OVER 15 ...

By Calum Ross on April 5, 2017

I have been in the mortgage industry for over 15 years and been investing in courses to help my improve my client process and customer service since day one. I really wish these books had existed when I first started as they would have put me light years ahead a lot sooner. This is a must read for anyone who wants to build a meaningful client centred profitable business in the industry.

GREAT REFERENCE TOOL. CONCISE READ. HE PRACTICES WHAT HE PREACHES.

By Amazon Customer on April 19, 2017

I just finished reading volume one. As a new broker, it was an easy read that does not make too many tasks to focus on and makes getting started achievable. Dustan provides great tactics and I will definitely be using this book as a reference tool and will be reading it again.

I am truly motivated between the support of my brokerage and the series and I'm looking forward to reading volume 2 and 3.

GREAT FOR NEW BROKERS—MAYBE SHOULD BE ADDED TO THE MORTGAGE LICENSING COURSE IN ONTARIO!

By Amazon Customer on November 5, 2015

Thank you Dustan! Finally, someone has written a book about starting out as a broker in Canada. Our market is a bit different then the U.S.

This gives you great insight into becoming a Mortgage Agent in Canada. 80 hour weeks! Dustan lays it out clearly and honestly. It is a great read from start to finish. Two things standout - 1. Dustan tracks everything, stays in touch, and is out there - 90% retention rate - wow. 2. Contact Cards - again - vital to staying in touch and keeping a database. It shows you that it is vital to have and use certain tools such as Excel, CRM and different apps that are available today....You must spend a bit to get set up but where can you get into a business for 2 or 3000 dollars with the potential to earn more than a doctor or lawyer...This is a business where you are always learning.

BUY A BOX!

By Jay Seabrook on November 13, 2015

★★★★★

A first class read written by someone who truly walks the talk and who also learned each of these valuable lessons hands on.

If you're considering being a Broker of any kind, this book is an absolute must read. All Brokerage Owners, Managers and Mentors should really read this and consider purchasing a box to hand to everyone who is looking to join your team.

Psyched about Volume 2 and 3!

AND THIS BOOK COULD NOT HAVE COME AT A BETTER TIME FOR ME

By Sara Lussier on September 27, 2015

★★★★★

I have been licensed as a broker for 6 months now, and this book could not have come at a better time for me. Be The Better Broker is jam packed with information about how to grow my business, and how to do so efficiently. This book includes marketing ideas, books to read, and tech gadgets that will lead me to a successful career in mortgage brokering. I highly recommend this book, and I am looking forward to reading volume number two.

TOP MORTGAGE BROKER SHARES HIS SECRETS FOR SUCCESS

By Ross Taylor on October 11, 2015

Who would have thought a niche topic like becoming a better mortgage broker has the potential to be a best seller? Yet, I have no doubt that is exactly what Dustan Woodhouse has created here. I envision most major Canadian mortgage brokerage firms making this series of books required reading for all aspiring mortgage brokers.

In fact, I only have one 'complaint', and that is I wish Dustan had already written volumes two and three of this captivating series.

There are so many takeaways from this book, it is hard to come up with a list of the highlights. But for me, they are as follows: Chapter 4 is called "Three things we wish we had known". Here Dustan asks twenty one brokers to identify the top three things they wish they had been told before taking the course, let alone entering the business.

A recurring theme from this chapter; indeed throughout the book, is that our industry is generally woeful when it comes to preparing newbies to be successful in the real world of mortgage brokering. With respect, the licensing course is a formality, and does nothing to ensure success in the real world.

Mentoring is hugely important, yet is rarely seen and done. Dustan laments "the fact is that currently the industry lacks robust training."

The bulk of volume 1 is mostly about Dustan's tenets for personal success. He generously shares all the little things he does routinely which collectively add up to make him a super-focused, highly disciplined sales machine. He might object to this characterization, as he repeatedly emphasizes it's all about doing the right thing for the client, and success will follow.

It's not necessary to replicate everything Dustan does – some of it may not feel comfortable or natural. But clearly he is not simply stumbling along in his pursuit of greatness – he has a plan, a vision of who he is, and how he wishes to be perceived, and his actions and approach to his business are all consistent with this.

Another recurring theme is about self-discipline – in today's techno world, so many of us allow ourselves to be distracted throughout our day. Twelve hours at work may actually only translate to a few hours of productivity. Personally I feel this is a societal problem – certainly not limited to mortgage brokers. Dustan has mastered his own domain, and he is correct it is a huge area for improvement for practically all of us.

I came into the industry a few years before Dustan, yet his achievements make my own pale in comparison. However,

I feel inspired by his writing and sincerely cannot wait to channel the knowledge he plans to share in volumes two and three.

LOVE HIS DEDICATION

By Gary on October 2, 2015

Dustan's truly a professional! He's put in way more than the 10,000 hours commonly need to Master an area of business. Love his dedication, and his devotion to his clients and the effort he puts in to his business. In business, it's all about adding value to the public and he's clearly done this with this book!

CONTENTS

#THISISBROKERING

STOP!

Do not pass GO.

Read This Complete Passage.

Until you have ticked each of the boxes below, you are wasting your time proceeding any further. At the very least you simply will not get maximum bang for your buck without a firm foundation.

For some this book may prove to be the "silver bullet," but you will already have done a significant amount of work setting the stage for success in advance.

In fact, if you're already feeling successful, but can't seem to break through the plateau you've hit for the past few years, this is the book for you. That plateau may be 50 files, 70 files, 100 files, or even 200 files. I myself was stuck at ~170 files for four years running before making a 25% jump to 237 files.

All that's ever stopping us can be found between our own ears. Writing this book has helped me rewire, and reading it will help you rewire.

If you are brand new to the business, hoping to short circuit the entire process by skipping the first three books and just reading this one — bad idea. You need to start at the beginning, go back to volume 1 of the series and work your way to volume 2, and then 3. Either read or ***listen*** to them. (Audiobooks are easy and www.audible.com has been a game-changer for me.)

Start with the list of books below. You too can power through at least one audiobook per week, and the mindset this list will create will prime you for what this book is going to ask of you.

And if the list below strikes you as an overwhelming task then just stop — stop here and shelve this book. Save yourself the time *spent*. However, if you are prepared to invest, not spend, invest the time reading this book and accepting the balance of tasks, checklists, and challenges within these pages, then carry on.

Game on!

Because as it turns out, breaking through a barrier requires planning, it requires mustering of resources, strength of character, stamina, and to quote one of my favourite authors when it comes to the topic of change, the most crucial thing of all is to have an inexhaustible supply of "***Discipline & Pigheaded Determination.***"[1]

1 Chet Holmes, *The Ultimate Sales Machine: Turbocharge Your Business with Relentless Focus on 12 Key Strategies* (New York: Portfolio, 2008).

I know that some of you just want the secret recipe, the shortcut, the aforementioned silver bullet. But you don't need me to tell you that the "silver bullet is bullshit"—you already know this. But if my life depended on delivering all that you need to know in a single word, it all boils down to the same thing, every last business, self-help, personal development, etc., book all distills down to one key word:

ACTION!

Your new reading list:

- *Be The Better Broker* – Volume 1
- *Be The Better Broker* – Volume 2
- *Be The Better Broker* – Volume 3
- *The Ultimate Sales Machine* – Chet Holmes
- *Relentless* – Tim S. Grover
- *Do The Work* – Steven Pressfield
- *Deep Work* – Cal Newport
- *The New Psycho-Cybernetics* – Maxwell Maltz and Dan S. Kennedy
- *Ego is the Enemy* – Ryan Holiday
- *ReWork* – David Heinemeier Hansson
- *The Rhythm of Life* – Matthew Kelly
- *Pre-suasion* – Robert Cialdini
- *Buddhism for Busy People* – David Miche
- *Mindset* – Carol Dweck

Now, sincerely, close this book here and now; complete the above reading list and then, *and only then*, pick this book up again.

You will be primed in a variety of ways to pursue a greater level of achievement for all the right reasons, or at least reasons that feel right to you right now.

I'll meet you back here shortly.[2]

GO!

2 I tuned back into each of these books all over again in order to get into the frame of mind I felt important for the creation of this book.

ACKNOWLEDGMENTS

The preparation and ongoing revisions of this series of books has involved countless conversations with dozens of people both inside and outside of the mortgage industry. The content has been improved and shaped for the better thanks to the input of many individuals. As an author, or just as a regular guy, expressing gratitude always worries me because when making a list of all the key people, can it ever really be 100% accurate? And truthfully my concern is as much about forgetting a key name or three as it is inadvertently adding a name and drawing attention to them in an unwanted way.

I remain ever aware of the fundamental law warning us of "the unintended consequences of the best of intentions," and so I offer the following thank you.

The list includes my family, both close and extended, as well as key people at both the franchise and head office level, many head offices, in fact, several underwriters, BDMS, VPs, and senior staff of various lenders, insurers, networks, media companies, professional associations, multiple appraisers, lawyers, Realtors, and, of course, many fellow Mortgage Brokers and Mortgage Agents. Significant input has come from conversations with fellow members of the Mortgage Professionals Canada board of directors, and most remarkably from a multitude of individuals spanning a variety of roles with a variety of networks and independent offices, including senior management of many of these offices as well.

There's been many a helping hand along the way, and I've tried to keep the finished products as non-denominational as possible. These books are a testament to the fact that the only way forward for our industry is to share. Share skills, share knowledge, share methodologies.

Share.

Share.

Share.

And share some more.

The level of sharing within our industry is akin to no other than I have seen.

As we stay divided so too do we stay conquered.

The above statement applies, from what I have seen, not to our industry but certainly to that of Realtors. As an example, I've routinely gifted copies of Gary Keller's excellent book *The Millionaire Real Estate Agent* to new Realtors who come into my orbit. More than once, this has triggered an angry call from an office manager (seemingly stuck in the Stone Age) upset over my sharing excellent data with their team on how to become a successful Realtor. Why? Simply because the book was written by the owner of a competing firm. How short-sighted can a person be?

This is right up there with Brokerage owners who try to limit their Brokers' attendance of industry conferences due to possible exposure to recruitment efforts of competing companies. Such managers need to ask themselves how truly weak their value proposition is to their agents that a highball and an hour's chit-chat at a hotel bar could break a relationship. How blind to the information age can a person be?

People don't leave companies, people leave people. Just as people don't join companies, people join people. It's all about the people, not the brand.

Keep this in mind as you build your brand. Because you are your brand, every conversation, every act of kindness, every gesture of goodwill seen and unseen all contribute to the building of your brand—which is to say the building of your personal reputation. Because there really is no "brand," there is just who you are as a person.

#Strongertogether

We should be proud of our industry; thousands of us have seen the light, we have seen the future. We are working together, we are collaborating to reverse the current market share split between Brokers and bankers from 30/70 to 70/30—maybe then we can call it a game of "every-Broker-for-themselves" (hopefully not). But for now, our best efforts are our shared efforts, and our biggest wins as an industry will be our collective wins.

Too utopian for you? Don't worry, things will get a lot more blunt and brutal in the pages to follow.

Look for lines like, "Vacations are for the weak," "Voicemail is for losers," and one of my personal favourites (OK, they are all my personal favourites), "The only economy that matters is the one between your own ears."

This series of books is a labour of love. There is no angle, no profit motive, and there was no grand scheme or master plan. There is simply a love of seeing people be all that they can be, a love of business strategy, and there was a clear opportunity within our industry to write a book and make my mom and dad proud.

But the real opportunity that this process has uncovered for me is the opportunity within each of us to be better today than we were yesterday, and to work hard today on setting ourselves up to be better still tomorrow. And so to those of you that have become my inaugural coaching clients, I owe you a debt of gratitude as we have both learned from each other, and much of this book would not be possible without the time we spent together.

To all of you who have allowed me to pick your brain on policies, procedures, best practices, and performance numbers—a huge THANK YOU!

You are the reason our channel will continue to thrive and survive. Keep on doing what you do so well.

Stay awesome!

A GUIDE TO MAXIMIZING THIS BOOK'S CONTENT

Based on feedback from readers of Volume 1, 2, & 3, the format of this book has shifted in some important ways.

1. The number of books referenced remains reduced as compared to Volume 1. If you are looking for some quality reads that influenced the creation of this book and the previous volumes, then I invite you to connect with me on www.goodreads.com where you can track what I am currently reading and share with me what you are currently reading.

2. Another service to consider signing up for is www.audible.com, which I use for tracking and downloading audiobooks. You will also find this series of books available there.

3. Ideally, you have a hard copy of this book that you can dog-ear, highlight, and write notes in the margins of. There is value in doing this with many books, in fact. I've gone away from adding blank pages at the end of each chapter as was done in earlier print runs. Instead I urge you to keep a journal, either written or digital, and write/type and store your thoughts and new ideas generated as you progress through this book.

4. I often buy books in all three formats: Kindle, paper, and audio. I like to Tweet or email myself passages, which is easily done via Kindle. It's also my preferred tool for highlights, as they all become catalogued and easily referenced. A paper copy is often attacked with a pen, pages dog-eared to return to again and again. Ultimately, I love being able to listen to books while walking, cleaning the garage, driving, and so on. Depending on the content and the activity I am engaging in, I adjust the speed to 1.25, 1.5X or 2X speed. The audio version of Volumes 1, 2, and 3 were narrated by an expert,[3] one of my favourites in the industry, and the plan is for him to narrate this volume as well. Look for it soon on www.audible.com.

As always, I ask that you please email me any feedback on how to improve this book or the previous volumes. Please point out a confusing sentence, word, or typo. It is highly appreciated. Thanks once again for the assistance from key readers of Volumes 1, 2, & 3 for the feedback that helped improve those books and this one.

Thank you.

3 Sean Pratt has narrated more than 900 audiobooks including some of my favourites—*Relentless* by Tim S. Grover being a current top five of all time.

"Attitude is everything."

—PHILLIP CROSBY

"Million dollar ideas are a dime a dozen. The determination to see the idea through is what's priceless."

—ROBERT DIEFFENBACH

"I fear not the man who has practiced 10,000 kicks once, but I fear the man who had practiced one kick 10,000 times."

—BRUCE LEE

INTRODUCTION

Will this book give you an edge?

Yes.

Top performers leave few books on their specific field of expertise unread.

Volume 1 is a primer on the business of Brokering. You read it, passed a copy on to a friend contemplating becoming a Broker and set them straight. The book sets out a variety of habits to adopt in order to build a foundation before entering the field, habits that many long-time Brokers find value in revisiting.

Volume 2 picks up on day-one as a licensed Mortgage Broker and adds several more key habits, best practices and scripts to the mix ¾ along with sharing some valuable and expensive lessons I've learned along the way. You've laughed and nodded in a few spots because you've been there with your own friends and family's files. Nonetheless, there were still a few new lessons in there that saved some files, and saved some face.

Volume 3 felt like a textbook, I know. All those scripts, scripts, and more scripts. You took those scripts, refined them, improved them, and mastered them. Made them better, made them your own. Your technical game is tight, you are focused, you are confident, you know your numbers, and your clients see you for the expert you are. Efficient and effective.

Nice, life is good.

But you want more.

Not more money per se, not more “stuff,” not more clients for the sake of having more clients. You want to process more, do more, be more. You are wondering how far you can take this thing.

This book focuses on change.

Internal change.

As you read the following pages, here is a mantra for you: ***How you do one thing is how you do everything.***

This can be a harsh lens through which to view one’s actions and parts of our lives, in particular the garage, fridge, closet, workbench, or storage room, but it’s a beneficial mantra because it forces us to pay attention to the small details ¾ the sentence structure in an email, the accurate date-stamping of documents, the extremely detailed explanations of mortgage terms that some clients require.

As you read through these pages, ask yourself if you are truly going the extra mile on each and every file. As I wrote these words, I asked myself this question more than once and have in turn upped my game with clients over the past few months.

Always be improving.

Always be awesome.

Mortgages are a commodity; trust is not.

The mortgage business isn't about "sales"; it's about trust. Clients have already been sold on a home, or sold on whatever they need to refinance for, be it a wedding, an investment, a new business, or a new boat. What clients need is less "selling"; what they *require* is more than just "financing." Clients require, and deeply desire, *guidance from an expert.*

I'm a Mortgage Broker by trade, an active and passionate one... or I was when I wrote most of this book. At this point (Spring 2019) I find myself President of a network of 1,300 Brokers & Agents responsible for six billion, closing in on seven, in annual funding.

Regardless, 1,695 mortgage transactions later, I know that in the mortgage business, enduring success is found one way only: by positioning oneself as *the expert.* A critical mantra; "I advise, clients instruct." At no point am I *selling* anything. This positioning (as the expert & trusted advisor) speaks to clients' deepest needs, the need to feel safe, not "sold."

Perhaps the Mortgage Broker's true product is the relationship itself. And this is where you try to tell me how "it's all about selling yourself," and again I would say that this is where too many of us miss a critical point: if you are recognized as, and referred to as, the expert, the trusted advisor ¾ then there is no selling to be done.

Emotions...ick.

Emotions drive 100% of decisions, thus emotions drive 100% of business. You may disagree with this sentiment at first, accepting only that emotions drive personal relationships. What else is business but a network of personal relationships? Anything less is a recipe for a business that will not last. Learning to control your own emotions is vital. After all, in any negotiation the one who speaks (a number) first is often the one who loses. This is because the one who speaks first is speaking from a place of emotion. For instance, you fear (an emotion) losing the business, losing the client, and so you cut to price.

As Murray Smith has said, "*In the absence of value, everyone defaults to price.*" True story, Murray, true story.

Controlling our emotions adds value in a wide variety of ways.

And although emotions play a significant (100%) role for clients' decisions, your own personal emotions must be held in check. As an infamous boss of bosses once said, "It's not personal, it's just business." It *is* highly personal for the clients, but you cannot allow it to be personal for you. Stay cool, stay calm, stay collected.

This book is full of strategies that will help you be the steady, dependable expert your clients need at a highly emotional time.

Only put off until tomorrow what you are willing to die having left undone.

—PABLO PICASSO

CHAPTER 1

THREE SIMPLE RULES

"The reason why worry kills more people than work is that more people worry than work."

—ROBERT FROST

In business and in life, three simple rules will take you far:

1. Be nice.
2. Work hard.
3. Maintain control.

Print the above three points out in large font and stick them above your monitor, mirror, or wherever they need to be to provide a constant reminder. (When working with our fellow humans we often need this reminder.)

1. Be Nice

The practice of being nice starts when you open your eyes in the morning, utter your first words, or dash off the first text, post, or email. Part of being nice is knowing when you may not be in the best frame of mind, and limiting people's exposure accordingly. If you are a grouch in the morning, then limit your interactions by rising well before others in your household and getting settled before engaging online. The same rules apply at the office. Consider resetting your voicemail on a daily basis with a greeting that states the day, the date, and the time after which you will be returning calls. This morning my voicemail greeting was, "Good morning, it's Friday, August 31 and I'll be returning calls after 11am. Thanks, have a great day and I'll speak to you soon." If you are going to adopt a daily updated voicemail message always record the night before as your voice will be smoother and also your memory sharper. It's all too easy for the first half of the day to slip past without remembering to update.

Once engaged at the office and answering your telephone, as well as responding to texts, emails, and other methods of inquiry, be prompt and be polite. Slow down and word your responses carefully, with consideration for clarity, and always with the understanding that this is what you are truly getting paid to do. Communication is the very essence of Brokering. Be calm, be clear, and be nice.

My standard client text response, saved as a shortcut, is, "*Thanks for your text. Due to regulatory requirements, all written communications re: your file must be done via email. Please copy*

& paste and re-send your message to dustan@ourmortgageexpert.com—Thank you for your time. Dustan Woodhouse—Mortgage Broker

Take it a step further throughout your day. Hold doors, put on a fresh pot of coffee when the office pot runs low, smile, and ask people, any and all people, how they are doing. Be the ray of sunshine in other people's days that you desire in your own. Smiles, much like yawns, are contagious. Skeptical? Is everyone around you a grouch? Ask yourself if you were scowling first. Make a social experiment of this theory. When next standing in a crowd or a line, alternate between a yawn and a smile. Smiles ripple further and faster.

A nice work-life begets a nice home-life and vice versa. Strive to be a pleasant person to those you love, and to those whose business you love. This will pay dividends in both of your worlds.

Nobody wants to work (or live) with a cranky or rude individual. In fact, people are 92.7% more likely to entrust a nice, yet inexperienced, person with their financial affairs over a grump with a wall full of credentials and awards.

OK, actually that last statistic is completely fabricated, yet if your perception of this author so far is that I am nice, then you likely trusted the 92.7% statistic. This is a key point: humans will usually, albeit sometimes mistakenly, trust *the nice* over *the rude*. It's how con artists ply their trade with success, often returning to work the same person multiple times.

However, simply being nice is not enough in business. There needs to be substance behind the smile; be nice, but also be skilled. This is a winning combination.

The next two points are all about the substance.

2. Work hard

You need to understand what hard work is before you can lay claim to having done any. Working hard should not be confused with work that is hard. Changing out tires on heavy-duty equipment is physically demanding; performing neurosurgery is mentally taxing; being an ice-road trucker with two sets of log books and a fierce drug habit in order to facilitate 24-hour driving shifts is hard both mentally and physically—but none of these examples gets down to the definition of hard work that applies here.

Author Cal Newport draws further distinctions around types of work in his book *Deep Work*. Mr. Newport refers to "shallow work," i.e., work done amidst all sorts of distractions without careful consideration or complex training. And then there is "deep work," which is work done with laser-like focus. This is protracted work solving complex problems, developing detailed solutions to complicated scenarios. Work that is done in an environment of limited distraction, and to limit distraction is critical in mortgage-world.

To work hard is to *work focused.*

To work hard is to *work efficiently.*

To work hard is to *work effectively.*

For effective hard work, you must choose an environment that includes a dedicated office outside of your home. Challenge me all you like—on this we can agree to agree that I am correct.

"Oh but that costs money," you might say.

No. *Not* having a dedicated office is costing you money. Tens of thousands per year, maybe more, depending on your profession.

But you "love the flexibility of 'working' from home." Well here's the thing: you are not *working* from home; more likely you are *kind of sort of working.* Only the rarest among us can achieve true dedicated focus for any duration from within a home office. Don't assume you are that rainbow-spitting magical unicorn; you are not.

Before you write me hate mail about how much you're crushing it from your home office, think about what your production level would be if you were in a professional office environment that we tailor-made for you together. To be clear: this is not to say that you would be happier, or have greater "balance" (whatever that illusion is), this is simply saying you will be more productive in a professional space. Production — that's what we are talking about here. Not balance.

Although to be fair an office outside of the home just might be exactly the thing to bring you closer to balance. An office within a home is an office located in the epicentre of any and all other distractions that you could possibly have in your life. Garbage to take out, a doorbell to answer, laundry to do, a dog to walk, a cat to feed, a shower at noon, or 3pm, or 6pm. Snail mail to sort, a dishwasher to unload, a pool to clean, a lawn to cut, some pictures to hang, a neighbour to chat with, kids home from school mid-afternoon to greet. The diversions pulling the home-based worker away from deep thinking are endless.

In a proper, dedicated office located away from your home, there is no TV, no talk radio in the background. Distractions are minimized. There is a phone that lights up, or at worst vibrates, but is otherwise silent when a call is coming in. All devices, including your computer, operate in total silence. No notification alerts, no chimes for email or IM. No audible alerts of any kind.

In fact, ideally there are no speakers connected to your computer. You will not be watching YouTube clips, surfing Facebook, or online shopping from this computer. The exception to this is Alexa—she is nice to have around. I find myself asking Alexa all kinds of questions because it's easier than opening a new tab to Google how long it will take me to get to Waterfront Station, what the temperature is currently, or maybe to play me a little thinking music (Mozart) or some writing music (LCD Soundsystem) on repeat.

Your work computer, found in your dedicated work office, serves only one purpose: performance of tasks dedicated to the completion of files. That's it. Personal pics, personal docs, personal social media surfing are all done from another device, a device not located in your office. In fact, wipe the Facebook, Instagram, Pinterest, Bumble, Thrinder apps from your phone; you will be glad you did. Actually, while you have your phone out, do the following:

go to *Settings* > *General* > *Accessibility* > *Accessibility Shortcut* > *Color Filters* then press the home button three times to enable grayscale, and to revert back click it three times again. Distraction factor reduced 10X.

Create a mental shift between devices.

Personally, I use a desktop PC for work, because PCs are not about having fun; they're all about getting work done. Sorry, Apple, but your ads backfired. I *want* boring and dependable, I want Excel and do not want a super-duper graphics card. Not in the office anyway.

Home is where the Apple (everything) is. The PC in my office equals protein and heavy lifting. My office is where I make my gains, and home is where I rest and recover and ultimately express a different kind of creation, often through writing. Each environment is increasingly about optimizing my performance in specific ways.

Your office will have a door that closes. Use it. Privacy is a vital component of focus, as is cutting yourself off from the office rambler, the doorway-leaner, and the got-a-minute meetings about nothing. Y'know the people who seem to think work is summer camp and want to interrupt your work since they have none of their own to get done.

This is your office. You are there to work.

Work.

Hard.

3. Maintain Control

Focus first and foremost on maintaining control over the one and only thing that is in fact within your control: your reactions. Learning to control your reactions is vital, and no matter our age, all of us generally need continuous work in this area. I'm 47 years old, and I am working harder than ever on this, actually not just on controlling reactions but more generally the emotions behind the reactions. Actually accepting and letting them out to roam free once in a while, but that's another book for another time; in this book, and in this business, during office hours there will be no free-range emotions. There will be calm, controlled reactions, and better still rather than being just reactive, we will be proactive.

We will better manage our clients by way of tuning into their inflection, tone, word selection, and pace of conversation, in turn, adjusting our own tone to defuse stress rather than inflame it. Mastering our reactions is the first step in mastering communications.

Never lose sight of the fact—and it is a fact—that clients

involved in any aspect of a real estate transaction tend to be of one frame of mind: *stressed.*

They may be young, nervous first-time buyers who are also planning a wedding and finding themselves pregnant with their first child. They may be move-up buyers with young children or teens, and perhaps another (surprise) child due any day. They may have a mortgage renewal due while rushing to leave town for their annual three-week vacation. Or they may be in a financial pinch, trying to leverage money from their home to keep a struggling business afloat, recover from a bad investment, or deal with a personal family challenge.

Many clients are stressed to the breaking point during the financing process and often feel as if everyone around them is pressuring, pushy, picky, and overly demanding in general. Topping it off, as with most things financial, clients also rightly feel that everyone involved in the process is speaking a needlessly complex foreign language. This is a recipe for disaster.

When clients are on the ragged edge of self-control, your poise, your confidence, and your aura of calm is paramount. You need to be that port of calm in a storming sea of confusion that is all things real estate.

Grant your clients safe harbour; alleviate their concerns.

Stay calm.

Calm is contagious.

Purchase control over parts of the process if you can—not illicitly, but by taking control of the related relationships involved in the transaction. Here is how...

Financial Control

Too many people in a commission-sales environment think of their compensation as their paycheque. Worse still, they view any expense related to completing a transaction as an attack on their personal bank account. This is short-sighted.

Here is a new way to see things. Imagine, if you will, that you are running a business. Guess what? You actually are! And as long as the business survives, so do you. So stop imagining—because this is reality!

Commission cheques are your company's *gross* revenue. Each cheque represents a sale for the business, not for you personally. Can you think of any company out there that has zero operating expenses? Zero marketing budget? Zero R&D allowance? Zero breakage, shrinkage, or write-downs? Of course not. Every business has expenses. Every business allocates or invests a percentage of its revenues in each of these areas and more. There is no such thing as a 100% profit margin; that is an employee mindset, and you are not an employee—you are an entrepreneur.

Every business "buys" business. Be it through marketing campaigns, referral fee programs, discounting the final product, we all buy business somehow, some way. Often we think that our way is "superior," when, in fact, it is simply different.

So how will your business (you) buy business?

Through control.

Control over staff, production, delivery, marketing? Perhaps, but ideally through control over the process.

Where are the weak spots in your process? Where is the opportunity to invest a portion of your revenues into the process to better control the outcome? Often, a weak spot is the clients' final signing of legal documents, done with a lawyer of the client's choosing. And what sort of detailed, comprehensive selection matrix did the clients use in order to select said lawyer?

Price.

Price, as always, is the default all too many of us tend to utilize. What do you get when you shop on price? *You get what you pay for.* Except in this case you get what the client paid for, and many times it's one raw deal.

What sort of madness has somebody simultaneously spending and borrowing hundreds of thousands of dollars in a complex transaction and then basing their selection of professional representation on a savings equal to or less than 0.0001% of the purchase price of the actual product in question?

Perhaps unsurprisingly, the client's final choice often results in a less-than-optimal experience for them, but often for myself as well, with their chosen legal representative making disparaging remarks about the lender, the term, the rate, the product, or even the Broker themselves, with absolutely no perspective or understanding of the complete file in question.

Strictly speaking, a lawyer's role is not to advise the client on the mortgage itself, but simply to confirm the client's identity, witness signatures, and confirm that the client understands the nature of the documents being signed and then to register the mortgage and title accordingly. The uninformed opinions of an outsider not privy to the entire client profile are less than helpful, in particular when they come from an individual who is *perceived* by the client to carry more authority than the Broker themselves. All too often these frustrating interactions sour the client's experience, tarnishing the transaction and devaluing the Broker's expert advice.

Always be careful who is having the last word with your clients.

Take control of your clients' experience from start to finish. Identify a law firm with satellite offices all over town, ensuring convenience for all clients. Consider offering a subsidy, no matter the file size, by an amount that not only bridges the price gap between the cheapest and best firms in town, but actually goes $100.00 further. This provides clients with the best advice, and a great deal. And it results in far fewer fires for you to put out.

This specific control play was critical in our growth and it greatly reduced headaches for all involved. Was this a $250.00 attack on my paycheque? No. This was a $60,000-per-year line item on our business income statement. We are running a business; so are you. Act accordingly.

Time Invested

Sometimes increasing control takes time, not money. I've known more than a few car salesmen over the years, but there are only a handful I can still name 25 years later. One is Wayne Marks. What did Wayne do that implanted his name so deeply in my brain? Was it billboard advertising? The Yellow Pages? Bus benches? Newspaper ads? An amazing social media presence? Door-to-door mailers? It was none of these expensive and ineffective things.

Wayne simply made a point of calling both my wife and I—calling, not texting—and wishing us a happy birthday. Cheesy? Maybe a little bit, but most years he was kind enough to call me a few days ahead of my wife's birthday just to remind me it was approaching. This was classy, clever, and obviously endearing.

At that point Wayne had been in the business for decades, and was no doubt spending an hour or more every single morning making his birthday calls. He could've easily spent that hour the way the other salesmen did: standing out front smoking, sleeping off a late night, complaining about a sports team. This would not be Wayne's style. Going the extra mile is Wayne's style.

However you want to look at it, all top producers purchase control over their clients' experience. They either take over the cost of part of the process just to control who is handling it, or they invest more time than their competitors ever will making personal connections. This lowers their dollar-per-hour income, but this is not the perennial top producers' key metric. Being nice is their key metric.

Look long and hard at your client process: where can you invest time and money of your own to enhance and better control the outcome?

Now open a Word document and type these words:

1. Be nice

2. Work hard

3. Maintain control

Then hit print and put them up on your office wall.

I just did.

Go forth, be nice, work hard, and maintain control!

CHAPTER 2

THE KILLER APP!

> *"As to Bell's talking telegraph, it only creates interest in scientific circles, and, as a toy it is beautiful; but...its commercial value will be limited."*
>
> —ELISHA GRAY

The true killer app is what?

It's the telephone!

During the day-to-day operations of the mortgage business, little else beyond an old-school rotary phone is required to get business in the door. Whatever phone you are currently rocking matters far less than possessing the skills to rock each and every call. The latest technology will not change your business; the only thing that will level up your business is you and your use of the telephone.

Several Brokers have shared the following lead conversion stats:

Four leads.

Two applications.

One funded file.

4:2:1

Your own numbers are not likely far off from these, although a ratio of 1.5 applications per funded file is more desirable.

Processing 99.9% of initial client applications by telephone allows for high levels of effective efficiency. Admittedly, your definition of efficiency may differ from my own. Let's look to Wikipedia for some assistance:

> "Efficiency is very often confused with *effectiveness*. In general, efficiency is a measurable concept. Effectiveness is the simpler concept of being able to achieve a desired result."

The telephone, so often taken for granted, is the second-most powerful and efficient device a Mortgage Broker can employ for relationship-building purposes. It cancels out long drives in horrible traffic, getting caught in horrible weather, lost time spent looking for a parking spot, lost time waiting on late clients, lost hours conversing at length with 439 Beacon-score clients who failed to mention their double bankruptcy history up front.

With the telephone you have the opportunity to be the purveyor of something much more valuable than simple key points such as the maximum mortgage amount, projected payment amounts, and (arguably) on the spot interest-rate holds. You hold in your hands the ability to grant the caller the thing people most highly prize and most ardently desire: *human connection.*

The vast majority of callers to our office are people I've never met in person, and likely never will. My repeat clients, and often some of my strongest referral sources, are also people that in many cases I've not yet met in person. Some of these telephone-based relationships are several years old. In fact it is entirely possible that if I ever did meet these people in person I might not live up to the image they have of me in their minds — perhaps it's best at this point that we never meet.

Which leads to the answer as to what is ***the most powerful*** and effective device a Mortgage Broker can employ for relationship-building purposes: your personality, which is composed of your emotional intelligence. And your emotional intelligence is what will build lasting relationships. You cannot convey your EQ through a paper, PDF, or online application—*although in a way you kind of are.* Take some time and speak with the clients, wrap your proverbial arms around their situation, listen, understand, respond, and convey that you have a solution for their challenge. An application built by phone is a win for the clients; they were expecting complex forms and delayed appointment times. But no—you made it so very simple. And in doing so simplified your own life as well. Masterful!

In addition to offering a fast and efficient way of working, the phone is a referral-generating machine. Or it can be. But all too many Brokers suffer from call reluctance. "How do I get clients without cold calling?" is probably the most often asked question from Brokers.

COLD CALLING

Cold calling is not picking up the phone book and starting with the A's. That's just pointless; you do not have that kind of time to waste, unless you're 17 and living at home for free. Even then, why would anyone willfully choose such a painful process when there are so many superior options.

Cold-ish calling is something any Broker has to do, to some extent, at the start of their career—until they have a roster of happy referring clients—but call reluctance can be a career-killing phobia.

Why don't people want to call strangers?

- *They might be mean to me.*
- *They might be smarter than me.*
- *They might ask questions I cannot answer.*
- *I will feel small and insignificant if rejected.*

Maybe, but more likely...

- *I don't have my thoughts organized clearly.*
- *I don't have my scripts rehearsed.*
- *I don't have a clear agenda.*

The key to superior cold calling is pre-heating the call on your end. This is done by believing that you will know what to say in any situation to any potential client, something that comes only from experience. Because experience is what teaches us that it's OK to not have all the answers all of the time.

Much like jumping into a cold lake, first you should do some research. How cold is it? Are there any potential dangers just below the surface to be aware of? Research people before you call them. Never has this been such an easy thing to do. But don't get too deep; that will seem creepy. Perhaps refer to a LinkedIn profile and call to congratulate them on a recent promotion, award, or corporate move. The cold waters of the first calls are uncomfortable and generally no fun. However, soon enough you grow accustomed, you learn to think on your feet, and, yes, you even begin to enjoy speaking with strangers. So get on with it!

When asked how I built my own database, email list, contact list, etc., my answer is always the same: one call, one interaction, one concentrated effort at a time. It did not build itself.

Start dialling. But start with family, friends, acquaintances, former co-workers, and Facebook friends, and work your way out to complete strangers from there. Refining your scripts with a warmer crowd is a good thing. The distinction I make between cold and cold-ish is when it comes to calling Realtors. Realtors, while technically a cold call for you, are themselves true cold callers; in fact, many of the successful ones are power diallers, and thus they are often more receptive to your call than you'd expect.

Not to mention that Realtors are the fast track to what you are looking for. Live files, instant action. And building a script to get business from a Realtor has always been easy.

Feel free to use mine: "Hi, you may get lots of calls from Mortgage Brokers, but not like this one. My name is Dustan Woodhouse and I'm an unrepentant workaholic. I won't be asking you to coffee, lunch, golf, a hockey game, etc. No, I'll be here in my office approving mortgages, or making calls like this one. So when your current rep is on vacation, when they can't find a solution, whatever—pick up the phone and call me, Dustan Woodhouse. I'll be here...approving mortgages. I'm emailing and texting you my contact card right now. I won't take up any more of your time, unless you have any questions?"

Now go—call 80 Realtors per day! What else are you doing with your time?

Oh, and don't worry, people are going to call you too.

Or perhaps that has you worried?

Answering Reluctance

Arguably worse than call reluctance, yet just as pervasive in life and in business, is *answering reluctance*! Why would a Broker let an incoming call go to voicemail? Think about this: that new number on your call display—that unknown number ringing through—is a potential client. And *they cold called you.* They are being the brave one today! They have taken the time to speak with you, right now! Act fast as the moment may pass, and you may be passed over. Reward their heroic act with a fast answer, not with the cold shoulder that is voicemail.

In 2019, letting a call go to voicemail is akin to telling that person to take a hike. And, in fact, they will, right on down to the next Broker on their list. If this advice seems to conflict with earlier advice given, it doesn't. Yes you need to be "always on," but you also need boundaries or your business will consume your entire being. You need to be in the right headspace, ideally from around 8am to 6pm, or some similar range.

The bottom line is that the telephone remains the Broker's greatest ally, an indispensable tool. Use it as such!

Following are the five vital phone habits that make all the difference to a Broker's success.

Habit 1: Answer the phone. Every time.
Voicemail is not your crutch!

The only call that goes to voicemail, during traditional hours, is a call coming in while you are on the other line with a client. And while you are on the other line you are hitting a pre-filled auto text back to the new caller. You're engaged. And speaking of voicemail, as per earlier—you've updated yours with today's day and date, right?

Habit 2: Call back immediately.
Plant this image in your mind: every minute you delay is a $100.00 bill lit on fire.

Missed a call? *Call back instantly*! The Realtor gave the client three phone numbers. *Unless they're a super cool raving fan.* And the client is already dialling the next Broker's number.

What are you waiting for? Return that call, don't hesitate, don't waste time listening to your voicemail—hit redial and get on it!

Habit 3: Control the call.

Whether the call is incoming or outgoing, have a plan. Create templates or checklists for various types of calls. These will help you stay on point and ensure that you don't forget something important.

It's an excellent idea to write out scripts that accomplish various objectives. Cover the initial fact-finding questions, or address answers to commonly asked questions. Clients might not come out and actually ask every question on their mind, but a skilled Broker has a good idea what the top questions are and builds the answers into their own scripts.

Many of my own scripts can be found in various blog posts @ *www.bethebetterbroker.com*

Habit 4: Create contact cards.

Create a detailed contact card (Office365) for every single number that you ever call or that ever calls you: clients, lenders, underwriters, Realtors, prospects, law firms, friends, family, wrong numbers—*everyone*!

This habit is a success cornerstone. It prevents a wild goose chase in the eleventh hour of a transaction as you try to track down what at first seemed to be minor player in the file but now holds the keys to 'file-complete': It's the clients bookkeeper, accountant, home inspector, listing agent, lawyer, basically anyone and everyone with a fingertip on the transaction.

I mentioned this habit in Volume 1, have done 45-minute presentations on the topic, and have also posted videos on Vimeo regarding this small habit's big influence over your success; it's critical to adopt this habit.

Habit 5: Follow through.

During an initial conversation with a potential client, be quietly noting the details that go towards a complete application. Take note throughout the conversation of client comments around where they bank, where they work, what they do for a living. Partway through the opening conversation, the mortgage application will actually be at least 50% completed. At this point make an "instant-gratification" offer along the lines of "*with just a few more questions we will have a complete application that will allow me to confirm maximum mortgage amount and potential monthly payments.*" Once the call is complete, sometime prior to, send the client agreement and documents list email to the client, and do not make a credit inquiry without that signed agreement. Verbal is not good enough, an email authorization is too weak as well, no exceptions—especially for family and friends. This is business, it's not personal.

One reason I prefer this approach myself is that I'm saved the embarrassment of re-asking the client questions they have already answered conversationally with me just moments before. This is not just an embarrassment but possibly a relationship-killer. Any time anyone is asked a question a second time, it raises doubts in their minds as to whether you were listening the first time. Always be taking notes, on every call.

Ideally, at this point in the call we have delivered:

- A maximum mortgage approval amount
- The math around payment amounts (e.g., $490.00 per month per $100,000)
- Locked-in rate(s), though only discussed a *range* of rates if at all
- A complete list of any and all documents required for approval

Once the call ends there is still more follow-through for you:

- Hit send on the (client agreement) email to the client
- Complete their application—100% of the fields
- Create the client contact card in Outlook
- Add the client to your email list (that blog you finally set up)
- Thank the referral source (email, call, and/or a thank-you gift)
- Contact the client's Realtor, send them your contact card, and build one for them in advance
- Contact the listing Realtor, send them your contact card and build one for them in advance
- Send your contact card to the client(s), Realtors, and anyone else involved in the transaction via email and text

In the course of one phone call, you have now gathered enough information to initiate an application, provided detailed answers to the client's questions, created a detailed new contact card, and wowed the client with your immediate attention and knowledge of your trade.

Best of all, you did so without leaving your office and you are ready for the next caller.

But if that phone is not already ringing, then you need to start dialling and making the phones ring.

Voicemail

Here is the good news for you reluctant callers: seven out of ten calls that you make will go to voicemail. And if your goal is to make ten calls a day, even better news—those seven count!

And you can leverage referrals from a voicemail message, it's being done every day. The key is leaving a powerful voicemail message that positions you as the go-to for any mortgage-related inquiries in that person's life.

i.e., *Hey, (insert name), It's Dustan Woodhouse, your Mortgage Broker, we worked together on your mortgage last June when (insert name#2) was kind enough to introduce us. I just wanted to check in and see if you had any questions or concerns around your mortgage. I'm here if you'd like to chat, again, it's your mortgage guy - Dustan, 604.351.1253. Thanks and have a great day.*

CHAPTER 3

FOUR WORDS TO FORGET

> *"I've learned that people will forget what you said, people will forget what you did, but people will never forget how you made them feel."*
>
> —MAYA ANGELOU

There are four powerful words to *eliminate* from your vocabulary. Never forget that we are in the business of building relationships and these four words used on their own, or in various combinations with one another, are easily mixed into a toxic word-cocktail of the relationship-killing kind.

Promise

Liar

Assume

Sorry

The English language is made up of more than one million words, yet the typical English speaker uses just 4,000 on average. Of the 4,000 we currently use, all that is being suggested is to nix four of them. We'll still have 3,996 words left to use at our will.

1. Promise

Liars make the best promises.
—PIERCE BROWN

One should never promise anything in business, not ever. All too often the word "yes" is spoken by one party, yet the other hears the word "promise." When a frustrated client—a rarity in our office—utters the words *"but you promised,"* I know for certain they are incorrect, for I have eliminated the word promise from my business vocabulary. In fact, I've nearly eliminated it completely from my life. Let's talk business, though.

Business is simply not the most important thing in your life, and you are fooling yourself if you think that it is. Yes you may, as I have done for a few months here and there, wake each morning to a recording of the infamous *Glengarry Glen Ross* speech by Alec Baldwin. And yes your ring tone, as mine does, may alternate between Shia LaBeouf's motivational "Just Do It" snippet or a copy of the motivational sales tape from the epic sales film *Vacuuming Completely Nude in Paradise*. And perhaps you viewed the movie *Wall Street* less as the cautionary tale that Oliver Stone intended and instead as more of a "how-to-win" guide. This is all well and good, even if a bit over the top, but you would still be wise to eliminate "promise" from your lexicon.

No matter how stone-cold you may think you are as a business person, always ready to deliver the presentation, never missing a scheduled meeting, catching every closing call to be made—all of this can be out the window with a single phone call saying a family member has been rushed to the hospital. Even if you love only yourself, that call from the doc that something is up with you can have the power to derail you at least once in your career. And breaking one single promise can be devastating to said career.

"*But you promised...*" The words project an emotion-laden guilt that overrides the fact that you may well have had no control over the situation at hand. It could be a personal health scare, an unanticipated market reaction, or a sudden regulatory shift. It matters not why, only that it is possible, and probable, that for one reason or another something in the realm of the client's expectations will change. It happens. Life happens.

Clients will throw the word *promise* back at you with the hurt and indignant tone of a petulant child whose trip to Disneyland you've just cancelled—which, in fact, you may be indirectly doing.

The client is not getting their way and they want to assign blame, which is, of course, as natural a human tendency as is the avoidance of blame.

Instead of *promise*, consider using the word *commit* or something similar. "Commit" is, for myself, far less laden with emotional baggage. It feels more businesslike to say to a client "*I commit to you that I will do all I can to make this happen*," as opposed to a promise statement that will likely be interpreted as "*I promise this will happen.*" Making a *Promise* feels overly personal and is likely to be misunderstood. Whereas *Commit* still makes a powerful statement, one more easily communicated and more clearly understood.

The word *commit* is often used in reference to sport, in particular to making a valiant charge for the win. We commit to a challenging line down a mountain, we commit to a radical late-game play, and we all love a player who clearly commits during crunch time. Yet even when that player fails, we don't fault them for having made the commitment in the first place. Instead we respect them for their efforts.

We all have a hierarchy of commitments in life, and a business commitment is more malleable than a promise.

Remove emotionally charged words from your business vocabulary, the word *Promise* is all downside with no upside.

2. The (other) L Word

A storyteller makes up things to help other people; a liar makes up things to help himself.

—DANIEL WALLACE

If there was ever an emotionally charged word to take us back to base feelings locked deep in our childhood subconscious, *liar* would be that word. This is a relationship-ending label to assign someone if ever there was one.

Using the word *liar* is akin to detonating an atom bomb in the relationship, potentially peripheral relationships as well. Few will forget the moment of its use. No apologies, no grand gestures, not even the power of 1,000 "likes" on the victim's latest social media post will counterbalance the soul-splitting impact of this label. Keep in mind it is a label; in fact, picture yourself with a red-hot branding iron with the word cast into it—that is what you are wielding with this word, as it's far more than just a simple word.

Few among us would use this toxic word in print or even over the phone, fewer still in person, yet while gossiping among friends it will on occasion arise in description of a third (absent) party. When it does arise, its use paints a rather unflattering portrait of the person speaking. In fact, it may evoke sympathy for the (rightly or wrongly) accused.

Business is all about nurturing relationships. So lock away the weapons of mass destruction and get out the garden tools instead. Take the farmer's approach with your business. Focus on sustainability. Suffice it to say that keeping clients (and those around them) warm, fed, and happy is a far more profitable long-term plan than going for the jugular.

No farmer mounts the head of his prize bull, jersey cow, rooster, or hen on his wall as a trophy to be admired. Instead they keep them well fed, safe, and healthy, tending to their needs regularly. Even when they disappoint in various ways, even when they do something out of character.

Think like an organic farmer. Build lasting natural relationships.

On occasion you may need to tolerate a thick layer of fertilizer to keep things on track, but at least it will be natural fertilizer and not toxic.

The indelible impression you want to be making is of somebody that is tolerant, understanding, gracious, and forgiving.

It's as simple as answering this one question: do you want to win arguments, or do you want to win business?

We've all dealt with people who seem to see the world a different way than us, they may be willing to cut corners we would never cut, or unwilling to cut corners we feel are just and acceptable to cut; in any event, disagreement and a lack of harmony will arise regularly in our business. Be respectful in your framing of a disagreement.

And avoid this word that shall no longer be spoken.

3. Assume

> *Assumptions are dangerous things to make, and like all dangerous things to make—bombs, for instance, or strawberry shortcake—if you make even the tiniest mistake you can find yourself in terrible trouble.*
>
> —LEMONY SNICKET

Assume is a sublime and deadly word. Like slow-acting corrosive acid, the assumption(s) made days, weeks, or even years earlier are eating away at the underpinnings of the elaborate skyscraper of a file you are putting together. And it is often only at the very end of the process that the error of the seemingly minor assumption dissolves the foundation of a massive amount of work.

Who was it that made the assumption(s)? Was it you? Was it the client? Does it even matter?

No, what matters is this: who is considered the professional in the equation? Likely you are (or were). Who was meant to ask every question, cross every *t* and dot every *i*? The professional was. Invariably, these situations boil down to being exclusively your own fault. Of course our intrinsic nature is to paint the picture of this all being the fault of someone else, if for no other reason than to make ourselves feel better.

Snap out of it! It's not about you, it's about the client.

Get over yourself. Own the mistake, take the pressure from the client. Get on with finding a solution—a fast and appealing solution. Again, not one that appeals to you primarily, but one that will appeal first and foremost to the client. *It's all about the client*! You, your feelings, your needs: these are all secondary at best.

If you find yourself starting a sentence with the words "I assumed," just stop. Own the fact that to make an assumption is nothing more than to make an "ass" of "u" and "me." A major mistake in life and in business is to assume anything.

Ever.

Stop yourself before you attempt to blather your way out of responsibility. Consider the respect we have for one willing to accept blame, 100% of the blame. Accept and embrace the power that is responsibility. And henceforth assume nothing. Ask!

You will be a rarity in owning the error. Especially if it was not really your error to own. Think about it: there are errors lying around left and right in most businesses that nobody wants to take ownership of. They languish unaddressed, with clients being negatively impacted all the while.

Be the rarity, own the error. And you will find yourself a respected rarity.

4. Sorry

Never apologize, mister; it's a sign of weakness.

—JOHN WAYNE

Never lead with *sorry*; always think twice before using this word. Is there a better way to proceed? Can you (still) take a different path to render a *sorry* needless? Can you *show* that you are sorry with a specific action, rather than weakly using the word alone? Words without action are unimpressive. Actions, as we know, speak volumes.

Take action!

If we are honest with ourselves—a difficult task for most of us—we usually see the use of the "S" word looming far off in the distance. It's our lack of action, or specific actions, that have triggered the need to utter this word...and we saw it coming the entire time.

For a pessimist, locked onto negative aspects of everything around them, there often seems no other option than repeating this word or worse still assigning blame to others (shifting blame is not a way to avoid the word, that's the worst plan). There are people who have set their mental cruise control and climbed into the back seat to have a nap, then, sitting up and looking ahead they stare listlessly at a distant tree, simply awaiting the impact. Why? Because climbing into the front seat, take the controls, and taking responsibility seems like too much work and does not guarantee success anyways. Neither does doing nothing. Make the effort, the extra effort, in advance. Never give up! There is always a way!

One clear reality around having to use the word Sorry is that the use of one, or all, of the first three on the list was probably involved at an earlier stage. In other words, avoid using the first three and by design, you'll rarely have to use the fourth.

Look past the negative, deal with oncoming threats and problems quickly. Dispatch them as early as possible and move on to better things.

Forethought and action can often negate the need of a "sorry." Better a small swerve, a skidding stop and perhaps even a reversal than a severe, abrupt, and final stop.

Be forward (thinking).

Be thoughtful.

Be aggressive.

Be doing.

And only as a last resort, be sorry.

CHAPTER 4

DINE WELL, DINE OFTEN...ON CROW

Too often we only identify the crucial points in our lives in retrospect. At the time we are too absorbed in the fetid detail of the moment to spot where it is leading us. But not this time.

—JAY RAYNER

The previous chapter focused on four words to eliminate from your vocabulary; this chapter elaborates further on the why, and the how-to-proceed, of things gone wrong. Because sometimes you just can't prevent a situation where someone blames you for something rightly or wrongly. In either case, instead of passing the buck, ask to be passed the crow—and dig in.

Avoiding blame is pedestrian, it is anticipated by all, expected even. Be smart, be humble, be right—and on occasion accept being called wrong—and also, be paid.

"But I was right and they were wrong."

So what?

To win the argument, but lose the client, is a poor business model. Can you buy groceries with your principles? Not where I come from. If a client is adamant that you did not explain a $200.00 line item to them, then as far as they are concerned they are right and you are ripping them off. Arguing will not help you. Accepting and correcting the situation, *not the person*, just might. Just write the cheque and keep things moving.

This is not recess, this is not a schoolyard game, you are not a child. You are an adult, this is business, you're the professional. Act like an adult, act like a business person—not a petty person. Be the professional in the relationship.

The client's perception is their reality, and their perception is that you made an error, or worse an omission.

But perhaps first you have to address your own perceptions, which can be inaccurate in the heat of being challenged. You may well be certain that you are the walking, talking epitome of contract-reviewing perfection, an all-knowing, infallible documents-and-detail-recalling deity. An error-free zone of excellence—yes, that's who you are. And the human part of you simply does not want to accept blame for anything—ever. Hey, hold on a second, you sound just like your client. Uh-oh.

Take a breath. Take ten breaths; in fact, take ten breaths using the four-count inhale and the eight-count exhale method. In any event, pause, think, and compose yourself. Then calmly let the client know that you value their business and although you do your very best to go through every single detail of each contract every single time, allow that you must have (not may have) inadvertently overlooked this item. And focus them on one thing and one thing only "that you will make it right." Waste not one word on telling them how we got to this place; instead, focus all their attention on you as the person that has the path back to where they need to be. You are on point!

Head them off at the pass. Offer a credit, the full credit, the full credit with a bonus gift, before they even ask. You are not leading with sorry and then just shrugging it off; you are leading with an action demonstrating that you are sorry, without (yet) saying the word. Even if the cost of correcting this situation sets you back personally to a net of zero on the transaction, you are better off having a happy client telling a happy story about you than you are making an enemy of this client over a futile attempt to cling to a single commission. Set aside how you feel about them personally, as that can play havoc on a situation like this on occasion. It is about the file, not you, not them. Keep the file on track. That's what all the other observers of this process are watching as well, the file... is it going to complete? The referral partner hopes so, the Realtors, lawyers, the client, and deep down you all hope so. So make it happen! At any cost—any monetary cost, that is.

"Winning" an argument can be the most costly mistake of your career. I have seen the misguided attachment to an individual's personal "principles" trump all logic in a stressful situation and effectively end multiple relationships: the relationship with the client, the Realtors on both sides, the referral source, and previous clients referred by the referral source who were also friends of said clients.

Be focused on the client's happiness, not your own.

And always remember when eating crow, the bigger the bites you take the less you are able to say with your mouth so very full.

Break out the word *sorry* only as the cherry on top of all else that you are doing to make this right by your client. Take ownership of the mistake, remedy the situation yourself, assure the client it is being handled. Assure them verbally and in print if need be, and finish after all of these steps with a sincere apology. Start with action, finish with words.

Some readers will take issue with this approach; few of those readers will achieve the levels of business success that they desire. Their ego is in the way.

Win the client, not the argument!

CHAPTER 5

TOUGH QUESTIONS!

> *"If you don't have the confidence to ask, you will never have the confidence to convince."*
>
> —KALANTRI

Step up and do the difficult.

Ask hard questions, questions you may not want to hear answers to, questions your clients may not want to answer at all. Failure to get answers early on is a waste of your own time, but more meaningful still is the disservice you're doing the client. Get down to the core of the matter; no matter how challenging, there will almost always still be a solution. Perhaps one with a rate premium, or a time delay, but with the right answers to the right questions you can zero in on the right solution efficiently and effectively. Anything less than full disclosure has you flying blind, potentially in circles until you simply run out of fuel.

All too many beginner Brokers struggle mightily to keep a flicker of life in the most challenging of files. They don't ask the hard questions, they don't press for clear explanations of credit challenges, or income documents' discrepancies. The new Broker is just so darn excited to have a client, to have a file to work, that they themselves are often more desperate than the client to find a way to make it work. And in that fog of desperation they lose sight of the questions they should be asking, because they are afraid of what the answers will be.

Each step of the process is filtering, with finer and finer gaps to keep moving the file through. The file either goes the distance, or as many files do—it gets stopped partway. Your goal is as much to complete the transaction as it is to eject the client from the process promptly and smoothly. The deeper you get into the file based on false or incomplete data, the messier it will be to extract yourself. A fast *no* is far better than a *yes* that is then reversed into a drawn out, tedious, and time-consuming *no* a week later, just inches from the finish line.

Addressing difficult questions up front has significant value in the application process.

Don't cling to a file with a death grip, learn to let go. A clenched fist is incapable of grabbing onto new opportunities. The file (and the client) should be clinging to you, not the other way around. You are the professional in this equation, you are the one *who makes things happen*, not the one *to whom things happen*. Be a shark, prowling for a legitimate seven-course meal. Do not think like the pilot fish and make the mistake of thinking that the client is the shark and you are along for the ride, pleased to receive some scraps. When you adopt this mindset it keeps you focused on who is running the show. *You* are the conduit between the money and the client. *You* connect the two together, expertly. So be the expert, be the professional, and ask the tough questions right up front.

A critical example of delving into details early on is clarity on the origins of down payment funds. Be clear that lenders want to see a paper trail for funds dating back 90 days. Yes, there are lenders that operate on a 30-day history, or even less, but put the client through the basic filter first. Is there a story here that you might need the details on? Do you need to adapt and filter out lender options? Ask for the maximum, not the minimum, because in the 11th hour you may need the maximum due to a late-game lender change and buried within that extra 60 days of account history you may run into entirely new and unexpected challenges.

Variations on down payment proceeds that we've seen in our office include incredibly delayed (four to six weeks) wire transfers from family in France and Brazil; $75,000 cash deposited a few days prior to the offer being written—yes it was legitimate, it was money from a 450-guest wedding. We had to provide the wedding licence and a few other documents to complete that file. Time is your friend when complications like this arise in a file at the start, time is your enemy (you are your own worst enemy) when these complications arise late int eh file—because it's 100% your fault for failing to be thorough up front.

An explanation of any black marks on the credit bureau is also very important. A client may think the dispute with a cell phone company, parking ticket, or gym membership six years ago no longer matters. We know that it will be relevant. Address it.

The client will say, "but it was such a small thing," and your reply will be, "That is exactly the problem." Many people fail to understand that their decision to sign and then break a minor contract or borrow a small sum that they then got into a dispute over—usually one that had them valuing their "principles" over and above their credit rating for the sake of $35.00—is a flashing caution light to a lender. After all, what if the lender inadvertently rubs this client the wrong way? Will the client cease making payments to them? This is crucial to frame and present to a client properly.

The reality is that people who dispute a small debt payment, to their own detriment, are also likely to dispute a larger payment and continue the cycle of self (credit) harm. Mortgage lenders see this profile, and they do not like it.

The other hot-button issue arises when a client fails to disclose a past bankruptcy thinking that it's been over seven years so they don't have to tell you about it. Meanwhile the fact that they are 57 years old and every single trade line they have shows a maximum history of three years tells the real story.

Caution Around Scripts

Once while processing an application, the gentleman's credit report came up with an all-time low Beacon score. I could hardly believe what I saw. We are talking 100 points lower than anything in the previous 1,000 applications. I said softly to myself, "wow."

The client, sitting only a few feet away from me, asked what the problem was.

Still staring at the screen, I used a standard line of mine involving credit reports for the last time: "*Your credit score suggests you were voluntarily or involuntarily removed from society for a few years, like you vanished into a cabin in the woods.*"

He replied, "Yeah, it was involuntary...two years less a day" (a common prison sentence reference).

I turned to face the client, and took a look at the man before me and in a split second all of the pieces fell into place:

- Referred by a divorce lawyer who used to do criminal defence work.
- The client had mentioned that the young girl at his branch seemed too scared to tell him the truth about his chances of qualifying. Too scared to even speak with him.
- Six foot seven, 350 lbs., a granite handshake, with huge skull-shaped rings on every finger.
- Lots of black leather boots, jacket, chaps...
- His only asset other than the cash for down payment (which had, in fact, been in the bank for 90 days) was the Harley Davidson he had ridden in on.

The majority (99.9%) of my clientele are regular folks, living mundane lives like my own. They have families, careers, and are building towards a planned retirement. But every now and then one of those wonderful clients has a relation, a neighbour, or a friend from the past that they feel compelled to refer to me. I do my best to avoid such situations—we all do. But here I was, foot firmly planted in mouth...

Knowing how to extricate your foot and yourself from these situations is important.

"Well, sir, I am afraid with this credit history there is nothing I will be able to do for you until at least another five years have passed and all of this falls off the report." I further advised that during the five years, opening two new trade lines and using them with perfection would be crucial.

Will this gentleman return to my office? Time will tell. It's been five years now, I just might have to face him once again soon enough. In the meantime, I will enjoy the other 99.9% of people I work with.

While hard questions and hard conversations are important, it could be said that wording of your standard lines and standard scripts is equally important and well worth periodic review. Clients are unlikely to call you out over odd turns of phrase, but your friends or your spouse will not hesitate, so run some of the "scripts" you use past these people in your life.

The Competition

While reviewing the credit report, did you notice any other recent inquiries from additional banks, credit unions, or Brokers? Ask your client about those as well. Are they, in fact, already working with another Broker? If not, why not? If yes then you should politely answer any questions that the clients have, while encouraging them to continue working with the original Broker.

Professional courtesy is important in a small industry, especially one in which consolidation is constantly occurring. Today's competing Broker could well be tomorrow's managing Broker.

If the competition is another channel, perhaps a lender that we do not have access to, then "game on." But if they are working under the same brand as you, or worse still, out of the same office as you, then think twice about doing head-to-head battle with a brother- or a sister-in-arms. What would be the point? Take the high road.

In the end it is the client who dictates what happens next. If the client advises you not to communicate with the previous Broker, and not to pay the other Broker any kind of commission split (*I've made contact with and paid a commission split to many competing Brokers over the years whenever the client allowed me*), then you must obey the client's wishes and deal with the other Broker's perception of the situation when and if it arises.

Do not disclose the name of any client to anybody ever. Not without the client's express permission. This policy may result in the other Broker being aware that their client has opted to work with you instead, and following the "be the vault" policy will restrict you from acknowledging this openly to the other Broker. If the client is dictating that there be no communication with the other Broker, or compensations split in any way, ask that the client not mention your name to them; do what you can to maintain good relations wherever possible.

Things are rarely as simple as they seem in this business. As few businesses involve such deep trust with such significant commissions.

Do the best that you can to make things right, or at least right-ish, whenever possible. Giving up 25%, 40%, or 50% of a commission to another Broker might not be something that the other Broker would do in the reverse situation, but it's not about what the other Broker would do. *It's about what you do.*

Ask tough questions.

Make tough calls.

Enjoy easier days.

CHAPTER 6

SCARE THE TOURISTS!

> *"Truth builds trust."*
>
> —*MARILYN SUTTLE*

You cannot help everyone you come into contact with, but you should always try.

Focus on solutions for the client, not solutions for yourself. At first you may find fewer paycheques for yourself with this approach, but there is also less stress. There is less stress working with a solutions-focused agenda because your days are spent putting square pegs in square holes and round pegs into round holes. There is no forcing things (just be getting paid).

If you have not yet scared your prospect away with the aforementioned tough questions and deep dive into their lives, then you have one last chance to do so. The final test to filter out an uncommitted client is the ever-growing list of required documents. The worst mistake is to go easy on a client with a "documents-lite" version of the master list. Inevitably this leads to a mad rush for "just one more document" in the final days leading up to completion.

In this deadline-driven business, we must rely on our client to supply significant documents well in advance of deadlines. You know what's needed; the clients do not. They are depending on you to manage them accordingly. Ask early, ask regularly, and ask for it all—until the list is complete.

Put all communications in writing on this topic for maximum clarity and a documented history. Use email, not texts. Maintain clarity about what is required, clarity about when it was first asked for. Always work from a master template that includes tips and tricks on accessing and forwarding documents. Go the extra mile and strive to make what is an often cumbersome and unfamiliar part of the process feel as smooth, secure, and efficient as possible.

Request an introduction to the client's bookkeeper or accountant to help expedite the process and remove some of the stress from the client's shoulders. Always CC the client on any polite reminders, and on your repeated thank-yous to keep communications clear and open. Keep in mind that every single person you interact with is a potential client and/or referral source. They are not meant to do your bidding; *you are meant to do theirs.*

There are two sorts of people in your orbit from here forward:

those who are doing business with you, and those who will soon realize that they should be doing business with you. Stay focused on this mindset.

When it comes to effective document collection, the number-one client that we all fail miserably with is a friend or a family member. Somehow we think that getting their ID, their void cheque, the innocuous bits and pieces is OK to delay, delay, and delay some more. We tease individual documents from them one by one, like slowly peeling off a bandage it's painful for all involved.

The slow peeling of a Band-Aid is the worst method. Perhaps you recall, as I do, how Mom was so very sensitive and would ever so slowly and tenderly peel a bandage from your knee, empathetically wincing along with you the entire time, all in an effort to cause what she thought would be less pain. Then Dad would appear out of nowhere like a ninja assassin, poke you in the ribs with his left fingers, draw your attention to the ceiling with his right, and then while you are wincing and gawking upward he would yank the bandage from your knee in a split-searing-stinging second. At least that's how I recall it being done.

My experience, and more importantly the science,[4] backs up the claims that a swift, painful jolt is actually less stressful than a long, slow, sympathetic process.

4 Dan Ariely, *Predictably Irrational: Revised and Expanded Edition: The Hidden Forces that Shape Our Decisions* (New York: Harper Perennial, 2010).

Just stop. Stop treating friends and family differently than regular clients, or stop working with them. Refer them out if you cannot put on your game face.

Buckle down, be forthright with all that is required, lay the big list on any and every client up front and get it over with. If they run screaming from your demands, at least they ran screaming up front, and not partway through the process as you "one-more-documented" them to death.

The days of quoting a rate during the first phone call are long gone anyway, as are the days of gauging the odds of an approval for 90% of clients on that same opening call. What of the remaining 10% of first-time callers that we might actually be accurate with? Even based on our experience and skills profiling applicants, the reality remains that in this brave new regulatory environment we don't really know a single thing with any certainty until we have the required documents in hand.

Which leads to the crux of this chapter, a phrase I heard first from one of the brightest people in our industry, Bernadette Laxamana: "No Docs No Talk."

Be blunt.

Be bold.

Be purposeful.

CHAPTER 7

HORSESHOES AND HAND GRENADES

"Close only counts in horseshoes and hand-grenades."

—*GRANDPA*

Close doesn't count in Brokering. Quality Brokering is built on precision. Specifically, precision communication.

Speak the language of your clients, within reason. Express yourself clearly without using one-hundred-dollar words when a one-dollar word will suffice—er *do.*

Use the power of story-telling to get your points across; it can be one of your own authentic and personal (real estate related) experiences, or one of a previous (always unnamed) client. Stories help clarify the what, the how, and most importantly the why.

Always ensure that the stories you are telling have a happy ending. Nobody wants to sit down to review their mortgage approval and then during the insurance portion of the process hear a detailed account of some other client's tragic circumstances. As effective, bracing, and true as the story may be, the clients will never forget how they felt during that meeting with you. Always keep it light, upbeat, and even a little quirky. Work with complete stories that wrap themselves up with a positive outcome, if not the perfect fairy-tale ending.

Few things in business can be sorted out with vague generalities, and the devil, as they say, is in the details. More accurately, the profits are in the details, profits are derived from happy clients, and no clients are happier than ones that feel like they have learned and have a better grasp of the process than ever before.

Referral math:

Happy + Educated = Referring.

In our business, there are a vast number of nuances around processing of files, which can, and often do, result in significant variations in profit per file. Despite the complexity of each transaction, one theme shines through all of this: happiness is built on clear communication, clear communication early in the process, and often throughout the process.

Such clarity is often arrived at via defined dollarization of a topic. When discussing interest rates, pause and ask the client which number matters more to them, the interest rate or the actual dollar amount that will leave their bank account every month?

Yes, the interest rate dictates the dollar amount, but here's the issue: *math is hard*. And whether you find math hard or not, most people just don't want to go the extra distance and do the calculations. Take the extra few minutes to do the math and convert numbers like interest rate and amortization into actual payments for the client to consider.

Ask a client if they can afford 4.45% when they thought they were going to get 3.34% and you will get one reaction, likely a negative one. Ask that same client if paying $1,500 per month and actually getting the money they need to make things happen works for them and you'll get a different (more positive) answer almost every time. That's a difference of about $180.00 per month payment-wise on a $300,000 mortgage at the aforementioned rates.

A difference of just $2,160.00 per year to own a home.

Own.

A.

Home.

These three words are perhaps the most powerful in the English language, because in most English-speaking countries these three words, "Own a home," conjure up visions of stability, happiness, a loving partner, smiling children, backyard

BBQs, extended family gatherings (extended family driving away from your home, far away to their home), and a host of other warm, fuzzy feelings.

And for that stated income client, who is running a landscaping business, the extra $2,160.00 per year was the equivalent of one extra job completed to make their home ownership dreams a reality for their family. The rate was a problem, until they realized the rate is not what's drawn from their bank account each month, the payment is. And they could (easily) afford the payment. The turn the conversation took from interest rate to actual payment is what ultimately allowed the clients to make the decision to move forward and embrace all those dreams attached to these three words: *own a home.*

For the Broker, however, all of this boils down to is a single word: *dollarize.*

Dollarize everything.

Clients want answers, and you're only going to deliver real answers, precise answers, answers that matter. Answers calculated and converted into monthly (or accelerated weekly) payments based on a full documents package and credit bureau as per the previous chapter.

Be prepared.

Be precise.

Be on point.

CHAPTER 8

BE COOL, FOOL

"You cannot shake hands with a clenched fist."

—GANDHI

Let's revisit control, with a focus on self-control. You need to invest time and energy into understanding why you react the way you do to certain stressors. You would be wise to study such topics as the brain (ideally your own), meditation, sleep science, and physical health. Understanding the dynamics that drive your own moods and decision-making powers will allow you deeper insight into the decision-making process of the clients with whom you interact with on a daily basis.

Start with any one, or more, of the various personality tests. You might think you know who you are, and you might think these tests are akin to a tarot card reading or numerology. And you may be right, I don't really have a firm opinion on the science of it all. I just know of my own experience, which includes going for a card reading and checking out numerology. Yes I'm the consummate skeptic, but skepticism does not mean you have to cut yourself off from new and interesting experiences.

I enjoy my search for self-knowledge and always seem to be gaining new insights on why I do the things I do, why I react the way I do, and in turn I am learning to refine my reactions to better suit my surroundings, my profession, and my personal goals. An added benefit of this insight is that it allows one to better understand, and accept (which is far better than tolerate), the actions of others.

Know thyself.

Spend a few dollars—spend a few thousand—on the study of your inner self. Check out the DISC personality test, the Myers-Briggs test, the Gallup StrengthsFinder2.0 test. Do one, both, or all three (or more) and compare the results. Spend the extra dollars on the detailed assessment and opt for an in-person review if you can. There is gold in this research. Learning how others perceive you can be eye-opening.

My own DISC test suggested that people under moderate to extreme stress (nearly every client who enters a Mortgage Broker's office) tend to perceive me as domineering, aggressive, controlling, etc. Basically this report suggested my clients might perceive me to be an overbearing ass. Not great news.

Just when I thought I had found my calling, and was truly helping people—apparently I was instead offending people with my approach, the irony being that my desire to win is actually a desire to see *them* win. Refinement of my personality was in order (it still is).

The MBTI suggests that I myself am an "INTJ" (Introverted, Intuitive, Thinking, Judging)—or as one online comment around INTJs suggests "an introverted jerk of a man." I'll let you Google the acronyms and follow up on the MBTI on your own.

Yes, I enjoy spending hours on end in my office alone working on complex problems and discovering elegant solutions. No, I'm not interested in a four-day-long beach party celebration of another year gone by. #nofundustan in full effect. What can I say? We all gotta be who we are.

Gallup results? I have yet to run this test, instead being focused on knocking out this manuscript—in 12-hour dedicated blocks of weekend time lost in my office and the process.

Once you know who you are, rein in who you are.

Be a little less of you, and a little more of your client. You may not be emotional, but allow your client some space to be emotional. You may not be hyper-rational and may cringe at having to prepare a spreadsheet for a detail-oriented client seeking amortization tables to the penny, again allow some time to prepare such documents.

Do what you can to adapt your style to match that of those with whom you are working. Once you are aware of the main styles that exist, you are able to understand the needs of certain clients faster and more accurately. You are also better able to see where the differences in your personality type will create potential conflict with others and you can avoid that collision with their fixed and conflicting personality traits. You will be able to do so before you have to break out the S word.

Forewarned is forearmed.

Be prepared for who you are, for who they are, and for how you are going to interact. Modify your behaviour accordingly.

CHAPTER 9

ONE OR ZERO...YOU DECIDE!

'Keep your friends for friendship, but work with the skilled and competent.'

—ROBERT GREENE

When hiring humans, the process can become overly complicated due to the undeniable 'human elements' involved. But we can simplify our decision making. Consider for a moment that we live in a digital world. A world of ones and zeros. Can we apply this binary logic to human interaction? Let's try.

Will you hire a One, or a Zero?

The decision is yours.

This is a deadline-driven industry, we aren't paid to sit on our hands, we are paid only for results, and results require action. In any business speed, focus and clarity in decision-making are vital. *Are you leaning forward, pressing hard, and taking action?* Or instead tilting back, coasting, hoping a problem (*a.k.a. opportunity*) will 'fix itself'?

Step 1—Assigning Values

This chapter is about who you ***choose*** to work with. Y*es that's right, you get to choose!* And some selections will offer higher value than others. Some will be a clear #1 and others will be... well, zeros.

1 = Yes

0 = No

Between the 'One' and the 'Zero' there are of course many shades of grey—fifty of them at least. But this is frank conversation on hiring humans. A conversation, and a formula, that eliminates as many shades of grey as possible.

It's worth noting that we tend to boil decisions down to three options, or three criteria, three metrics, three sizes of coffee, three men walk into a bar, three bowls of porridge, three strikes – you're out! We love our threes. Three is acceptable in many contexts.

When making a decision it's easy to keep three options in play: YES, *maybe*, or NO. In pursuit of clarity let's lose the 'maybe'. Let's lose the *mushy middle ground.*

Focus!

It is a heck Yes, or is it hard No?

Step 2—Applying Values

Get out that trusty pen and paper, start thinking, start writing. Write down the decision you are struggling with. Write down some pros, cons, wants, needs, etc. And then narrow it down to three critical criteria.

You get to keep just three points here; often people will have ten, twenty or seventy-two. Three is manageable for a decision. Drill down to your ***three non-negotiables***, the deal-breakers, the things that truly matter, because without these three you cannot proceed.

Label each as either a One or a Zero in relation to the job that needs doing. No middle ground here, no scale of 1–5, 1–10, or even 1–3. ***Be absolute***. Does 'x' truly matter? Does 'x' make the final cut?

Yes or No? One or Zero?

Re. hiring

My list & score:

- Punctuality 0
- Hairstyle 0
- Tattoos 0
- Skill **1**
- Stability **1**
- Commitment **1**

I am not super concerned about the first three items on that list myself. Seriously...please give me a chronically late, sleeve tatty'd, mohawk sportin' person with first-class professional skills, just two previous employers for the past 16 years, and a clear commitment to the work. *Pretty please.*

Having identified the three non-negotiables, we move past the petty nonsense of Walt Disney-style employment rules, and maybe, *just maybe*, we make a great hire.

First we do the math.

Step 3—Do the Math

For each potential employee, score them One or Zero for each of your categories. Then take your categories' values (1 or 0) and ***multiply*** them. Is the answer One or Zero? *Yes or No?*

Don't add the values together (1+1+0=2) and suggest '*two out of three ain't bad*' – ***multiply***. Always multiply, because if an applicant scores Zero for one item, then the answer re. hiring is Zero, a.k.a. 'No'.

> 1x1x0 = 0

Whenever there is a single zero the answer is always Zero ('No').

When it comes to our winning applicant, the three main criteria identified from our list above are:

- **Skill** – Are they a master? - **1**
- **Stability** – How long is their typical stay with a company? - **1**
- **Commitment** – Are they willing to sign a three-year contract*? - **1**

**Few employment contracts are enforceable per se, but the exercise of documenting expectations for both sides creates a common point of reference if the relationship gets rocky.*

Once again, the math – if an applicant's scores were 1, 1, & 0, then the equation would be 1x1x0 = 0. Again, just one Zero in our top three makes the final answer a ***Hard No***.

If our applicant is a zero in one category then they're a zero overall.

Only perfect candidates make the shortlist. As with our candidate above who scores a **'1'** in each of the three core criteria. And **1x1x1=1** – which also equals **'Yes'**.

Considerations

Too extreme?

Prefer to make exceptions?

How's that working out so far?

We are focusing on just three critical criteria for a reason. Toss away the exhaustive list of thirty-three criteria which comprise the 'perfect' associate. One cannot hold out for absolute perfection, you don't need perfection; you yourself are not the personification of perfection. But you do a pretty great job anyways, right?

Also you have a business to run, and chances are you've already left hiring way too late and are feeling '*way too busy*' to tackle this task as it is. So stop the radium, enough mental minutiae, keep-it-super-simple (KISS). Focus on three critical criteria and then apply a succinct Yes/No ranking to each.

Don't like their tattoos?

Get over it; it's 2019, even grandma's got ink.

Don't like that they are 15 minutes 'late' every day?

Get over it, they aren't late, they are consistent and that's valuable, embrace it.

Don't like X?

Unless X = one of the fundamentals...**Get over it, past it, through it, move!**

You've perhaps heard the old adage '*hire for attitude and train for skill*'. Forget this nonsense. This is truly the worst advice in the mortgage business because as mentioned above, most Brokers wait way too long to hire their first, second, and third associate.

Compounding this problem is that fact that we are all

delusional in that we believe we are somehow going to 'train' and shape these ice-cold rookies into the ultimate mortgage team. *Because why? Because how?*

KEY POINT: *What evidence is there to support the notion that you can train anyone?*

A wise yogi once suggested that it takes ten years to master a skill, and then another ten years to master *teaching* that same skill. Consider this very carefully before embarking on the path of training staff in the mortgage business.

Completing 50 or more files per year on your own means you are sort of...***OK—you are very***...organised, and likely also an unrepentant workaholic, which is fine—it is perhaps better that 'work' is your vice than the other options; you're my kind of people. However, unless you get truly lucky with that first hire you are going to stall out, flame out, and maybe burn out. It may take 15 years, but eventually you will get there.

What about me, what was my approach? I got super 'lucky' with my first hire and we cracked 160 files in our first year together and shortly after we pushed past 200 files per year, continuing to work well together for ten years (and counting).

LUCK IS NOT A STRATEGY

Part of my 'luck' was having a trusted third party introducing us. That third party advised each of us that the other was solid. That we each knew what we were doing, that we were both good people who knew our business well. And so I hired a fully licensed underwriter that had been working with a top producer as associate #1.

I was referred by someone I trust to an expert. I hired an expert, paid accordingly, and benefitted exponentially. Leverage your professional peer groups as much as possible to find that expert. Do not try and build an expert from scratch. You don't have time.

To think you will offer detailed and effective training to a rookie in the midst of 100-file-years...please. *When will this training happen?*

Which two hours per day for the next six months are you going to block off for this new task?

Here is your new mantra when it comes to hiring:

HIRE FOR SKILL, AND TRAIN YOURSELF TO DEAL WITH THE ATTITUDE.

Applying the One or Zero, the In or Out, the Yes or No mindset takes discipline, *but it is a useful discipline.* It's not about having every last piece of data; it's about highlighting the main three decision points and being unwavering on them.

This method of decision making is supported by a much smarter man than I, one Nassim Nicholas Taleb, author of *Antifragile.* He suggests that to make a decision or take action on a topic, one needs no more than ONE good reason. In fact, *adding reasons* to a solitary **good** one suggests weak resolve and works against the initial rationale.

As an example, let's consider marriage.

Do you need to create a spreadsheet for such a decision? If so, you may be the least romantic person on earth. Let's hope your soulmate is also prepping a comparable spreadsheet, because that's all that will save your robotic bacon if said spreadsheet were discovered.

When it comes to marriage a solitary reason, albeit sometimes an unreasonable one, will do:

LOVE

There is no room for shades of grey here; the score on this criterion is either One, or Zero – *Yes or No.*

Proceed accordingly.

To bring this back to business, you need only one material reason to *end* a relationship with an employee. It's often well worth ignoring the small things, the piercings, the collection of action figures all over their desk, their obsession with 'their' sports team; but do not ignore a *material* reason when it presents itself or you will regret it.

MATERIAL REASON: DISHONESTY

There is zero tolerance when a legal or ethical line is crossed. Never compromise your business, staff, partners, integrity, values, or self-worth for the sake of a single file. This is an 'all-caps' ZERO of a reason, and only a single Zero is needed to end the process.

As per the above formula:

Massive file = 1

Easy approval with documents in hand = 1

One piece of documentation is notably questionable = 0

1x1x0=0.

End it, end it quickly.

Move on to your next client. Be smart.

And if it was one of your staff that altered, or realised they were submitting altered docs, again that's a Zero in a critical category.

How you react, while under immense pressure yourself, to your employee's actions, or your client's actions, or your employee's actions in response to your client's actions is what separates the Ones from the Zeros. The onus is on you to be a number One! Every single day.

Conclusion

Your business is not built just on satisfied clients; ***your business is built on satisfied staff, referral partners, and industry alliances***. With the right team, the clients become the easy part.

Be a leader, *set an example worth emulating.*

When it comes to hiring and firing, same rules apply.

Be a ONE, be in the game, be on-point, every single hour of every single day.

CHAPTER 10

CRUSH YOUR ENEMIES TOTALLY

"On an important decision one rarely has 100% of the information needed for a good decision no matter how much (time) one spends or how long one waits. And, if one waits too long, they have a different problem and must start all over. This is the terrible dilemma of the hesitant decision maker."

—ROBERT K. GREENLEAF

The title of this chapter is "Law 15" from Robert Greene's enlightening book *The 48 Laws of Power.*[5] Mr. Greene's book is worth keeping handy for a time when you may be feeling overpowered and in need of a strong defense.

In conflict first ask yourself why, *why fight*? Ever. The goal is to never trade blows. However, if you must take an aggressive step, be definitive. End the confrontation in a single move.

5 Robert Greene, *The 48 Laws of Power* (New York: Penguin, 2000).

Invest 99% of your time in providing an excellent and informative experience for your client. The sum total of an effective marketing campaign in this business is summed up as "position yourself as the expert." Expert advice provided openly is a winning approach nearly every time. And this approach minimizes competition.

Conflict interrupts profit

There are times when into your orbit will flow disruption and competition. Any conflict via competition must be dealt with swiftly and succinctly. And such expedience is why just 1% of your time will be consumed with this sort of thing.

The following option for dealing with a common competitive situation can be used by Brokers in their first year or their forty-first year of business. It's no way to build a business, but it is a way to protect a client, your database, a referral partner, or a lender relationship.

In the early days of one's career, gaining experience is as valuable as earning income. Every file processed helps build experience and most importantly to build a database, as well as a referral network. Getting paid is important in those lean days for sure, but it is ***never*** the primary reason to process a file. The primary reason to complete any file is to build your database. The database is the origin of all referrals, and referrals flow best from completed files.

Experience and reputation are also valid reasons to complete a file. In other words, working for free, while never as exciting on payday, can still be very valuable. It may be about keeping the client and/or referral source locked in the mindset that you are always the one with the solution, because you are. So don't rule out the following strategy simply because it conflicts with your "principles."

Principle #1. Protect the database.

Nurture it.

Build it.

As a rookie progresses into their career, they will have enough consistent volume that it won't be about processing a file simply for the experience. You will have had plenty of that. But an industry veteran may wish to complete a file in the following fashion as a defensive move against another Broker making inroads into their referral network or into the industry at all.

The Scenario

You've invested many long hours and many late nights working through the client's pre-approval stages, the writing of an offer (perhaps several offers), the pressure of the days following the initial offer getting the lender's final approval, the processing of a vast array of documents, the lengthy explanations about the entire process, assisting the clients with commitment and compliance documents review, home insurance, mortgage insurance, solicitor selection, etc.

And after dozens of hours, maybe months of work, the client comes to you with, "Hey, I am not sure what to do here, but another Broker has offered us a rate X% better than what we have with you—*and it is from the same lender.*"

What now?

Apocalypse now? Go nuclear? No, don't do that, then everyone loses.

Don't push the button just yet.

Hold, hold, hold—inhale on a four count, hold for another four count, exhale on an eight count, repeat ten times...

Just breathe.

Calm.

Breathe.

OK, still with me?

Let's enjoy this moment of calm and seek some clarity with a quick review of this situation from the beginning;

Step 1: Did you do your very best to confirm with the client up front that you were the only person they were working with? Did you ask this question more than once, during the pre-approval and again once the offer went live? Did you make it clear that it is much like their relationship with their Realtor, i.e., clients do not hire three different Realtors to approach the same seller, nor should they retain the services of more than one Mortgage Broker to approach the same lender.

Step 2: Was the client unduly influenced by another source, perhaps their own Realtor, a family member, or their co-worker(s) pushing another Broker or a banker? Or was this something they came up with on their own?

The answers to these questions lead to a fork in the road.

If the situation is such that the clients were flat-out shopping you, hustling, just gaming for a rate to take back to somebody else to beat from the very start, well then that's not cool, and they are not worthy of this solution. You don't want them in your database, and you should've had better filters all along to eject them far sooner, like within the first 15 minutes.

As an aside: *If you feel compelled, by all means make it clear to the client that you could've written a "market-rate letter" up front (something I often do) for them to return to their preferred lender with. No muss, no fuss. Explain that this way we each would have only lost a few minutes of our lives to one another, rather than several hours, days, weeks—it's all about them and their time, of course (stick to the high road here).*

Clients that knowingly play games with your time must be set free. We specifically do not want referrals or repeat experiences from such clients. Clients are for the most part genuine and sincere in all that they say and do. You can't let one bad experience cancel out nineteen, or ninety-nine, other excellent experiences. Although doing so is human nature. One bad night with beverage "X" and we are off that drink for life, or often several years. One bad meal of a certain sort and that entire food group, or franchise, is removed from the options list. It's the same with clients; we get burned badly once and we are hyper sensitive for some time to come, which is toxic and must be fought off.

Breathe.

Take it down a notch and relax.

Breathe.

The odds are heavily in favour of the client having been coached by a third party and it's also highly likely that neither the client nor the third party truly understand the mechanics of our business.

Realtors are also often unclear that we get paid zero unless the mortgage actually funds through our office, and that it was us personally, not the lender, that prepaid for the appraisal. And that our own compensation is the least of our concern; we've simply been hustling hard to do the very best we can for the clients, because we genuinely care.

Not every Broker thinks this way, but you do—you wouldn't have read this far into this book unless you cared about improving your business model. And I wouldn't have written this book, or the other three, if it was all about the money. I've invested thousands of hours into the writing, re-writing, updating, fine-tuning, etc., and 10,000 copies later every expectation has been exceeded massively when it comes to connecting with other humans and helping them through various stages of their business growth.

And so we are people that like to go the extra mile, or three, and what follows is what I propose for the extra mile, in a specific competitive circumstance.

It is my belief that clients are virtually never the devious schemers we think they are; and so we move now into retention mode. As a previous chapter made clear: assume nothing. Above all, never assume a client is being untruthful. Calmly ask questions (verbally) and get to the bottom of how they came to have this second quote or approval from another Broker.

Is it an approval? Or is it just conversation? Keep in mind that clients will often jump ahead making assumptions of their own based on a single conversation with a teller in a branch.

But, if you feel that the other party, the agent, road rep, or Broker is truly a threat to your closing clients that you genuinely still want to close, then we proceed to step #3.

In my own book of business, the method that follows has only been used twice in more than 2,000 applications. If your up-front filters are not efficient, you'll find yourself in this position more often.

Step 3: GAME ON, FOOL!

You want to play?

OK—Mr. or Ms. "All-I-have-is-a-low-rate." Let's play!

For clients who got the unfortunate advice to engage another Broker, and to keep it all hush-hush, yet legitimately did not realize the extent of the damage they would be doing to a Broker's business through an unfunded mortgage commitment, for them it's going to be a great day. These clients will be smiling, likely still feeling a bit uncomfortable, but smiling in the end.

For the other Broker, the one who thought they would swoop in and scoop up that nicely wrapped file in the 11th hour after all the heavy lifting was done, those long late-night conversations already handled for them, the one, or five, other properties underwritten and cancelled due to failed inspections, or being outbid — well, for that Broker or road rep it's going to be a disappointing day.

For us, also a good day, a fun day, if not a terribly profitable day.

That's cool, because it is not about us, it's about the clients, the underwriters, the office staff, and all the people that help get a file where it needs to be—***File Complete!*** Personally speaking, I'm not so selfish, nor my principles so self-centred that every file need be "full-comp." In fact, low comp, no comp, and even paying out of pocket to complete a file may be more in alignment with our core principles than we first realize. It's less about love of the work than about love of the clients.

To let a file go in the 11th hour without doing serious battle is to disrespect the work of all the other aforementioned parties involved. You have your team's sweat equity to consider here, as well as your own.

And so here is what happens next:

- Your rate becomes the absolute lowest possible with a full buy down, ALL the way down. Use up the volume bonus if the lender allows it; you are looking to trade all the comp for a discount on rate here.
- Cover the client's appraisal costs, even if it hurts.
- Cover the client's legal fees.
- Offer to wash their car for them.

It's cool. I know this hurts, but we are in pursuit of something bigger than a single commission here.

The message being sent to the competition is that we will not lose our clients to them. Ever. They will not build a successful business with these tactics, at least not when competing with us. They'll actually need to build their business via skill, or poaching someone else's clients.

Recognize this "price-first" business model for what it is. It's been around since the dawn of time in every industry and always will be.

A point of clarity: *A discount brokerage, one that clearly advertises this up front, is 100% a business model I understand and don't have any issue with. A solidly profitable business can, in theory, be built on forty basis points. It's all about driving process* *and extreme efficiency, something that most Brokers are not even in the ballpark on.*

If I could attract files that involved less than an hour of client interaction, were AAA*, with zero pre-approvals being worked, and had complete documents packages in one email — well I'd do that all day long for 40% comp. Sounds great. And it's an easy plan to sketch out on a napkin, over a lunch or dinner, easy to sketch, but actually executing to a profitable scale remains elusive for most who've tried.*

When it comes to the clients themselves, few are truly comfortable using one Broker's services, connections, advice, availability, and skills and then kicking them to the curb after the dust settles for the sake of a few basis points on rate alone. Few humans are in fact wired to be this cold. Unluckily for us, current legislation (at least in BC) excludes any sort of exclusivity contract or charging of a fee for service.

When we cannot lock clients into working with us, and when all of our charm has failed, what are we left with? An approach that makes very little sense on the regular, but this situation is not going to be "the regular." This is a path very few files go down, so it works fine in small doses. The mechanics of the entire process must be clearly explained to the client. The clients understand that I am a full-service provider, and that is why I do not discount—quality is not discounted, sub-standard goods are discounted.

In this case the goods being offered by the other Broker are substandard. And that's why they are discounted accordingly. The other Broker is doing one-tenth of the work, and this can be mapped out for the clients, and they should see the value in what you have provided. But this is not vital.

Step #3 sends a clear message to the competition: "*You will not poach my clients, and I will do this all day long. Unless you step up and start earning your clients through expertise, you will not last.*"

How will I last? The expert always lasts.

Do what is right for each situation. And this situation, for me a 1 in 1,000 situation, this was right. Sustainable? No. But it does not need to be.

Do what is right by the client, by your business partners, and then, finally, worry about yourself. Because if you spend your time putting your clients' and your business partners' needs first, *your needs* will take care of themselves.

The time spent on the file, on the approval, and invested in the client is already lost, the commission is also already lost. It's all of your relationships that are now on the line. Time and money are out of the picture, all that is left is all that mattered in the first place: the people with whom you work.

Someone has come along and stuck a knife in your leg, leaving you two options: you let them stick you again and again until you can no longer go on, or you turn around and face them and say, "So you brought a knife to a gunfight, eh?!?" and then you pull out a rocket launcher and finish them off before they know what hit them.

Overcompensate.

CHAPTER 11

A FAST NO!

"When you say no to the wrong people, it opens up the space for the right people to come in."

—JOE CALLOWAY

One way in which our industry tries to force the issue of loyalty is through the use of exclusivity agreements (in the jurisdictions that do allow them). Realtors are able to use them, commercial mortgage brokers typically use them, and in some provinces, *not all*, legislation allows their use in some residential mortgage transactions as well. In residential lending, these contracts, designed to bind clients to a single Broker no matter what may come, tend to be a crutch and are rarely enforced to the letter. When they are enforced by the Broker, it's usually done out of emotion, not logic. After all, is enforcing a contract on an unwilling party a move that leads to repeat business, lasting love, or, most importantly, to referrals? Not likely. Is this any way to build a positive reputation in the community in which you live and work? Is it the path to long-term success? No. Conflict is not a business plan in this industry.

The first question to ask yourself is if your value proposition is so weak that you need a contract to force people to work with you? Are you so unable to demonstrate your value to a client that you need to lock them into a binding agreement? In more complicated and longer-term relationships there is, of course, great benefit to a contract. After all, this is what the final mortgage approval itself is, a binding long-term contract. Why not a contract negotiated in good faith?

Learn how to determine what is and what is not a relationship being built in good faith. Learn how to do it quickly. The most effective way is, of course, to lead by example and extend faith (your expertise) generously on the opening phone call.

In a commercial transaction the amount of time that can pass from start to finish on a file can be several months, sometimes years. A contract is important here. In a commercial transaction the compensation can be ten times, or even one hundred times, that of a residential file. And most importantly, the client is paying that compensation; it is money directly (rather than indirectly) out of their pocket.

The majority of residential mortgage transactions have a client relationship that is as short as ten days, and rarely longer than a few months. The average net commission rarely exceeds a few thousand dollars, which cannot logically be justified as worth pursuing in a court of law. The amount of time and energy spent on such a frivolous action is time far better invested in working on new files. Block the disaster file from your mind (save for the telltale signs that were likely there from early on in the file; those deserve attention, review, analysis and consideration in order to improve your process moving forward).

Perhaps I watched a few too many Clint Eastwood movies growing up, but I still take a person's word as their bond. If I look you in the eye and shake your hand on an agreement, that is as binding as—maybe more binding than—any contract from my side.

Have you positioned yourself as an expert? Such that people are clamoring to work with you? Are you having to turn down business? If so, you need no exclusivity agreement. On the other hand, if there are tumbleweeds rolling through your lonely office and you feel the need to grab the next client that comes through the door and handcuff them to you with a contract, then you need to ask yourself a question: *who hurt you?*

Seriously though, do more than just read or consider the following statement, think deeply on it and determine whether or not some wholesale change is required in your business and perhaps in your life:

The trusting are trustworthy, say the trusting and trustworthy. The untrusting are untrustworthy, say the untrusting and untrustworthy.

I think that I just came up with that now, but it might be a line out of some 1960's Spaghetti Western. I'll let you Google it.

When a client does break up with you—as most people who are chained down will try to do at some point—are you truly going to take them to court? Are you really going to incur the wrath of a publicly recorded dispute over your compensation? Or even more ridiculously over a $300.00 appraisal? Really? Why? To prove a point? Get a life.

Please consider carefully what it is about your personality that would drive you to drag out a negative relationship over months or years with court dates, rather than simply ending the negative relationship as quickly as possible and focusing your time and energy on building new positive relationships elsewhere. Is your drive to be right at all costs that strong? Are you throwing around words like *principles*, *promises*, and *liar*? We already know that two out of three of those words are meant to be eliminated from your vocabulary. And by now you should be catching on—certain principles have no place in an effective business plan.

Win clients, not lawsuits.

Also, hire a therapist. Sincerely. This is a way less expensive option and far more productive in the long run.

CHAPTER 12

DEATH BY TAXES

"A paradox of life. The problem with patience and discipline is that developing each of them requires both of them."

—THOMAS M. STERNER

One of the more insidious things to creep into a successful Broker's life, into the life of just about any and all commission sales agents who are "lucky" enough to be paid in pre-tax dollars, is the problem of tax planning.

Planning is not often the strong suit of the strong salesperson.

Specifically, planning to pay income taxes on time.

A casual conversation with a tax agent quickly reveals that the top group of people in tax arrears are not simply small business owners in general; specifically, the people in arrears are Realtors, insurance agents, and Mortgage Brokers.

Making CRA's hitlist; outlined in 12 simple steps:

1. Human Being (HB) starts a new profession.
2. HB struggles dearly for the first three years, incurring no income tax bills whatsoever.
3. HB has a breakout year and earns strong dollars.
4. HB, not having earned any taxable income for a few years or more, has no ingrained habit of setting aside X percentage of each cheque for future taxation.
5. HB arrives at tax-time following the breakout year with enough earning momentum into the new year to (mostly) address the previous tax year's bill on time or close to it.
6. HB's stellar income trajectory marches onward, income rises to wonderful levels (the tax burden is also rising, but is willfully "unseen").
7. All outstanding household bills are paid, a car or two is upgraded, perhaps a few other luxuries added to life. A renovation, a vacation, a few stay-cations, life is grand.
8. And still no habit of setting aside a fixed percentage of each commission cheque for income taxes is formed, the expenses of life expand to fill (gross) income allotted.

9. HB gets the tax bill for stellar year number two—and cannot come close to paying it off in time.

10. HB goes on a tax plan to pay the taxes due just in time for...

11. Year #3's tax time. Leaving HB perpetually indebted to CRA.

12. HB tightens belt considerably not only to pay off last year's taxes, but also set aside next year's in advance. HB's brain screams against this, perhaps the family members scream a little too.

HB and family have grown accustomed to spending it as it comes in. Saving is a new skill to learn, a new habit to form, one that they never previously had the luxury of needing to learn.

HB goes one route or another:

Option A—keeps on crushing it, earns their way out while living a frugal life and gets ahead of the curve. Two years of pain, and then relief like never before.

Option B—yields to the crushing weight of all the obligations and suffers a down market that stops the money train before they catch up with past due tax bills. HB's world is turned upside down as judgements, liens, garnishing of wages, and worst of all the judgement of others comes into play.

We are all HBs, so what to do? ***Option C*** is what. Start forming the habit of setting aside even just 15% of gross earnings in an account that nobody touches. This account has no cheques, no debit card—an account that is a true pain in the ass to access money from.

Live ahead of the curve. Live your life not one dollar at a time, live it 85 cents, or better yet 50 cents, at a time.

CHAPTER 13

AWARDS ARE WORKED FOR, NOT WON

"Awards represent achievement, and to an extent they show more about who you are as a person than the personal items you picked out and purchased, because they show desire, ambition, goals, and accomplishment."

—JAROD KINTZ

Industry accolades are nice; they feed the ego, and most people need their ego fed. By "most" I mean to say "me." Not you though, you are woke and have transcended the need for awards. But ego is important, because an ego too small will not serve as any kind of defense against the dark arts. I refer, of course, to the mundane insults and innuendo (often generated by self-talk) that we must deal with on a day-to-day basis. An outsized ego acts as a fuel tank for self-motivated drive, and while outsize egos tend to get dented a whole lot more than the smaller ones, it's the outsized ego that allows us to put ourselves out there in a variety of ways. So awards or otherwise, all of our egos benefit from some kind of attention.

More importantly, awards are accolades one can hang on their office wall, post on social media, and, if nothing else, they provide third-party validation to our clients and business partners as to how hard we work and offer a measure of the efforts we make each year. Awards provide clear communication to clients that we take what we do seriously, year after year.

People like to work with successful people.

People like to refer their friends and family to successful people.

The interesting thing about awards is that many people make the statement (even just to themselves): "I want to be nominated for an award." Yet this is the extent of their action plan, ending where it began, with an empty statement.

Imagine if, instead of vaguely fishing for assistance, you applied effort and engaged in active pursuit of a specific award. Let's start with an upgraded statement: "I will win X award!"

Accordingly, one should document the next steps to be taken to achieve this goal.

The list might look something like this:

- Determine all awards you qualify for.
- Contact the organizers to confirm qualifying criteria.

- Note deadlines and create a plan to meet the timeline.
- Confirm with organizers in advance that you will be able to attend the event no matter whether you are winning or not—be there if nominated!
- Make a list of all related parties to whom you have a strong connection. Related to the event (sponsors, organizers, attendees, fellow nominees, past winners).
- Make a list of all related parties to whom you have a medium connection.
- Make a list of all related parties with whom you currently have either a weak or no connection at all.
- Create a script to reach out to all three groups either in person, in writing, via telephone, email, LinkedIn inmail, or smoke signals—whichever feels most appropriate to each party. Let them know that you are in pursuit of this award and why their support matters to you, i.e., you respect them and their opinions.
- Look for opportunities to nominate any of the parties on these three lists for awards themselves—even if in your same desired category. And let these people know you've nominated them. (Personally I just quietly nominate—but this is not about me, it's about you). Make the effort to write said nominations for others. Reciprocity is a powerful thing.
- At the very least, endorse each person from all three groups of people on LinkedIn and, where applicable, write a recommendation.
- Ask your head office and upper management for any assistance. Ask specifically if you can be of service to them in relation to the event.

Winner, Winner, Chicken Dinner.

Congrats, you won. The work is not over here. Once you win an award, be sure to properly thank all those who had a hand in it.

Leverage it fully: social media, email signature, website, plaque on your office wall, etc.

But don't go too far, don't get theatrical; after all, it's still just business.

Awards are important, but still a very long way down the list of day-to-day priorities.

Awards don't generate new business to speak of; they are nice to have. They strengthen the ego, which as we know is vital in business.

If you truly want to feel good about yourself, take this chapter and apply it on behalf of somebody else. Write nominations for behind-the-scenes people who help you day to day, do what you can to see them gain recognition. We as Brokers tend to be in the spotlight and awarded most of the credit far too much of the time. As if what we do happens as a kind of single-handed accomplishment rather than what it truly is, the work of many.

It is the work of many.

Keep this top of mind on a daily basis.

CHAPTER 14

BUILD ON STRENGTHS, OUTSOURCE WEAKNESSES

"Everyone sees what you appear to be; few experience what you really are."

—NICCOLÒ MACHIAVELLI

"It is easier to act yourself into a new way of thinking, than it is to think yourself into a new way of acting."

—MILLARD FULLER

First-time recreational triathletes often make a common error: they over train in one area—usually their weakest. And for many confidence is highest on land, the run, and the ride, and disproportionate resources are expended on preparing for the swim.

The problem with shoring up one's weakest skill, in business, in life, and in a triathlon, is that a competitor can in fact appear weak in one area, climbing out of the water dead last, for instance, and then prove to be such a powerhouse elsewhere, such as the run or the ride, that they lock down an overall win once on dry land. So don't worry about achieving anything beyond baseline competence in your areas of weakness. Baseline competence in a triathlon swim = not drowning. In business you can outsource your baseline area(s) of weakness to experts, levelling up your entire performance. And, for me, when it comes to triathlons, when I can outsource the swim, the run, and also the ride to three unique powerhouses, that's when I'll enter a triathlon.

This tendency to over-allocate resources to our weakest areas often stems from one of the many things we are taught (incorrectly) from an early age; among other foolish things like "don't judge a book by its cover," and, "if you just practice this instrument long enough you'll learn to love it."

We are taught from an early age to focus on our weaknesses, and it took me a long time to realize that I do not have to master each and every little thing. These days when I find something that I'm weak at, I find a shortcut. I outsource it. In some cases the thing to outsource may well be something we are quite competent at, simply from a time/value standpoint. As we age, we tend to realize that the one thing we are going to run out of first is time, not money—money's the easy part. As we begin to value time over money, we learn to happily (mostly) part with money and reclaim time.

Allocate your resources (time & money) wisely.

Focus on strengthening your natural strengths.

Go for the gold, where you know gold can easily be had. Instead of spending extra time and money on training and coaching to improve a weak area that only represents a small portion of the overall effort, focus instead on perfecting your strongest areas.

Yes, we are talking business now.

Success in business rarely, if ever, flows from natural talent. Instead, success is most often the result of an innate expectation to be our better selves, and to improve something specific. Top performers play to their natural strengths—a logical approach. Top performers are driven to hone their skills constantly, to refine their processes endlessly. To apply massive effort in the development and application of skills.

I learned this, luckily, very early in life.

My experiences in school were perhaps ironic considering how I spend my days today. Grade 11 was on the semester system, giving us two shots at anything we failed the first time around. I had always been a C+ student (C+ students call a C+ "good enough") without ever cracking a book, but Algebra 11 proved my nemesis. Scoring just 48% (fail) in the first semester, I followed in the second semester with a 49% (another fail) and then—more due to a tolerant summer school professor than my own sudden keen understanding or increased study habits—**50%**, a pass.

At no point in my schooling would any guidance counsellor have predicted I would one day be involved in the financial services industry in a capacity that includes complex equations. Nor would they have imagined that I would, in my spare time, write blog posts containing a significant number of complex and detailed mathematics accurately worked out on my own.

How did this come to pass?

For lack of a better word, neuroplasticity. (I know this sounds like a one-hundred-dollar word.)

One may not be a "math person," but they can certainly be a "numbers person." Regardless of your success or lack thereof in high school mathematics, you can *become* a numbers person. You might think I am about to reverse course on my "don't pursue your weaknesses" comments; I am not.

Why are we weak in certain areas? Often due to a simple lack of interest or, more accurately, from a lack of understanding in how this thing will apply ever in our lives. Perhaps you also recall the grade school argument that algebra was "something we would never use," something for scientists, not for jocks, skateboarders, or rockers. Who needs that stuff! And to some extent I associated any sort of advanced math with people who wanted to split the atom, thus tuning out completely on the topic.

However, the year after graduating from high school I began operating my own business, and as it grew rapidly I quickly came to realize that all basic business, and many of life's decisions, were in fact powered by algebraic thinking. A light bulb went on.

I can recall sitting at my desk in my small automotive parts and repair shop in 1992 working out a scheme on a significant transaction and realizing that it was in fact a real-life word problem that involved more complex calculation than just "solving for X." And my interest grew in grasping such calculations for running and growing a business. The part of my brain that had been capable of advanced math all along finally lit up.

Because our brains are not hardwired, contrary to outdated thinking, we can, in fact, learn whatever we want to learn—provided we have enough drive and a genuine interest. It was a revelation and a confidence booster to realize that our brains are capable of taking us much further than most of us will ever go. We are all capable of so much more than we realize.

The critical factor is genuine interest. This is why a triathlon swim is so tough for so many. We can train hard, hire the best coaches, and buy the sleekest suit, but if at our core we hate swimming, hate the water, and hate the process of improving at it then we are limited from the start.

And so as my first business grew I analyzed and broke apart the business process, identifying various pieces that could be done better or more efficiently by others, allowing my time to be focused on what I did best (which was work the telephone) and the business morphed from an in-person local service shop into a mail-order behemoth. It was instantly apparent how much simpler a telephone transaction was as compared to the in-person process.

Focusing on the highest and best use of time is a strength in and of itself.

Invest in others who are better than you are at various tasks.

Build on your strengths and outsource to supplement the weaknesses.

A constant goal in my own life, one I will never achieve, is to become the best version of myself. This is one of those "it's about the journey not the destination" situations. The goal of the best version of ourselves will never be achieved, but the pursuit thereof should be the standard we set for ourselves.

Take some time to speak with people you trust, and to think and journal on identifying your own strengths. And then for a plan to level those strengths up.

I don't file my own taxes, keep my own books, or try to fix my own teeth. I retain experts for these things.

I also try to avoid cooking, cleaning, and, where I can, driving. These are things I am (mostly) competent at, but the time they consume is better invested in higher-value activities.

The focus of becoming a better me is achieved primarily by building on the strengths I already have. For instance, I enjoy public speaking, and so I take almost every opportunity to speak. But as much as I wish I could play the piano, I know that I will not allocate enough time to it, and so I do not fool myself by registering for lessons when I know I will never practise.

This mindset led me to take my first business from $30,000 gross with one employee (me) to $4,000,000 gross and fourteen employees inside ten years. This growth was fuelled by my continuous hiring of additional people to take on tasks that did not represent the highest and best use of my own time.

In other words, always strive to stay dry and never have to suit up for that swim at all.

CHAPTER 15

ARE YOU INTERESTED OR ARE YOU COMMITTED?

"It's a great advantage not to drink among hard-drinking people."

—F. SCOTT FITZGERALD

Sitting in a recent mastermind session, the comment was made that at a certain production level there no time left for fucking around, to which I added that one does not get to said level unless they stop fucking around.

And so with some hesitation I insert this rather personal chapter; it's not getting up on a soapbox here, this is just a slice of my own story. This is a book of new habits, new systems, and new viewpoints, of ourselves and of others. So take from these next words what you can apply as you see fit, however you can in order to remove an old habit no longer serving you and create the space for a newer, more beneficial habit.

Some of my more challenging habits to break over the years have been over-consumption of potato chips, then french fries, and more recently jujubes. Having just typed this last sentence my mouth is now watering and I want to take a spin down to the food fair or corner store. How easy it is to fall back into our old ways. Instead, I will take a spin to the gym.

On to the meat of this chapter, and feel free to substitute the word "alcohol" for something else in your life that you might do well to remove. Don't throw out the main point of the message over the details.

My main point? That 30-day challenges are for chumps. Thirty days is in fact a cakewalk for most of us. So step it up and turn it into a 365-day challenge.

Four years later, still not drinking, my one-year challenge may have turned into the rest of my life—as I've learned something truly valuable. I've learned exactly what sort of drinker I am, but that discovery took about 333 days.

What I learned about myself is something it is unlikely anyone partaking in a Sober October will learn about themselves (but kudos to the Sober October crowd—you have to start somewhere).

A confluence of circumstances one October brought me to a

point where I decided that one full year away from alcohol was an experiment worth embarking upon.

From a (late) decision to lead our then-teenage daughter by example, to solidarity with our teenage son who had made the decision not to drink as part of his personal training and competitive regimen, to a blog post about one year off booze (worth reading) by one James Swanwick, the bottom line was that on Sunday, October 5th, 2014, I pulled the pin.

When I quit, I really, really quit. I tend to hold myself to high standards in (nearly) all that I do, no more so than when public declarations are made.

Frankly, time flew, although not at first. At first it was actually a little bit disturbing. I'd gone six weeks without a drink many times over the years due to circumstance or choice. In fact, I'd gone six months at least twice. I rarely had even a single drink on a weekday, and yet the first six days of this challenge, five of them weekdays, were spent with way too much of my mental real estate occupied by second-guessing this whole quitting thing. The fact was, I could feel the weight of the specific tumbler in my right hand, swirling my right wrist to mix the two ingredients, Kahlua and vodka, known as a Black Russian. I could feel the cool texture of the beverage running across my palate, hear the clink of the cubes, revel in the manly burn of the vodka, the delicate and sweet aftertaste of the Kahlua.

I wanted a drink.

Weird.

Whatever.

One year.

Decision made.

Get over it!

Time accelerated, six weeks later it was no longer a daily thought. A few months later it was not even a weekly thought.

Then in a flash, 333 days later, or thereabouts, I was talking with my (then) wife and mentioned that it was only four weeks from the one-year mark and suggested we have a party, one at which I would light it back up again.

The response was surprising and profound; in an evenly measured tone she stated, "You shouldn't."

I asked for more than two words, and received five more that would set the tone for my continuing on this path:

"You're just better without it."

Well, what do you do with that? As mentioned, what I've chosen is to continue with this challenge as a key piece of the pursuit of my best self.

In hindsight, I was essentially a competitive drinker from my very first drink as a teen. I can still recall counting each one diligently as it went down. I never stopped counting drinks, even when I "grew up." As life progressed, so did the numbers, as if I was "winning" at some unspoken contest nobody knew they were in.

In 27 years of drinking, I was physically sick just twice, with a 23-year gap in between. Hangovers were rare and when they arrived were of little consequence. I seemed built with a high tolerance and serious stamina, and every few months would inadvertently find myself pursuing a new high score I would then retreat into semi-retirement and focus on other tasks for the weeks or months in between these one-night binges.

Which brings me back to the critical point: 30 days is not a challenge! Thirty days is a cinch if you are competitive.

In the excellent book *Relentless* by Tim S. Grover[6], a reference is made to one of the elite peak performers Mr. Grover trained, and Mr. Grover's concern about whether this individual had control over his drinking or the drinking was controlling his client. The individual, when challenged, responded that he would quit for 30 days, and just like that he did, and in Mr. Grover's eyes this proved the "control" was with the individual. With no disrespect to Mr. Grover, I would disagree with that statement, knowing what I now know. And I think his client might admit, in hindsight, he was fooling himself and his trainer.

What I realize is this: any one of us can quit anything for 30

6 Tim S. Grover, *Relentless: From Good to Great to Unstoppable* (New York: Scribner, 2014).

days. This is our nature. It's easy for us to simply immerse ourselves for the 30 days in other activities. We will hyper-focus on something else, all the while knowing in the back of my mind that a mere 30 days later freedom of choice awaits us once again. Thirty days is nothing for a truly goal-oriented individual.

And no doubt the athletes that Mr. Grover trained have far greater ability to focus on their goals than most of us. Focus matters.

Thirty days for a peak performer is a cakewalk. It is a short-term goal, easily achieved with little time for introspection.

The next time you set a goal, or a challenge is thrown down, don't just do the minimum required. To use Mr. Grover's terminology, the minimum is what a "Cooler" does. Hitting targets hard and breaking through them elevates you to "Closer" status, but to take a challenge and 12X it—that is something a "Cleaner" would do.

A Cleaner brings an atom bomb (himself) to a knife fight, not simply a gun.

So, will I take up my own challenge and 12X my original one-year goal?

I am already a Closer in some areas, why not push harder and be a "Cleaner" in this one?

Decision made.

CHAPTER 16

THE GROOVE IN YOUR BRAIN

"You're only as young as the last time you changed your mind"

—TIMOTHY LEARY

There are many grooves worn into our brains. The repetition of mundane tasks creates low-level grooves with low impact on our day-to-day well-being. However, there are other types of grooves worn so deep that even when trying to think or behave logically we either trip over them or, worse, we fall right into them, derailing whatever task or thought we were trying to complete.

There are the positive grooves and there are the negative grooves. And there are simple steps you can take to change them.

When we repeatedly tell the same stories, we forge a neural

pathway in our brain that causes us to feel a certain way about the people in our stories, the nature of the events, or the general topic at hand. These stories, often outliers of routine behaviour, can warp our view of the world and the people around us for better or worse.

Conversely, if we can let go of the negative experiences we encounter and embrace a bit of sunny optimism, then we just might have a positive impact on our productivity and that of others around us.

Case in point: a few months ago, I woke up at 4:45am—an hour and fifteen minutes before my standard wakeup time—to ensure I was in the office and prepared for a call that was supposedly important to the caller, only to receive an email cancelling, just minutes before the scheduled time. They were sorry, but they'd completely forgotten about the call.

My first reaction was kneejerk: complete annoyance. I wanted to send an email to the person explaining the lengths I'd gone to in order to accommodate said phone call. Y'know, tell them all about my first-world problems.

But why? Who would I be doing that for? While it's okay to feel annoyed, it's important to quickly get past the negativity. The reality is that I truly do not know what else is going on in that person's life and I ought to give them the benefit of the doubt, at least once anyway.

But here is the real question: Why am I retelling this story?

Because within a few minutes of my initial reaction I calmed down, sent an email saying something along the lines of, "No problem, I can fill this hour easily, have a great day," and I let it go and moved on. No hour, or day, spent ruminating, no time lost in a negative space, and no opinions formed about "people."

As soon as the call was cancelled, I instantly deleted it from my calendar, replaced that time-block with a new task and got busy making quality use of my "extra" time.

I also didn't bother sharing the story with anyone else. I didn't mention it to anyone who arrived in the office to find me there early, nor did I talk about it with my family when I returned home and they asked about my day.

I chose to ignore all of the standard chances to complain about the call not happening as scheduled in order to purge the memory from my brain.

At this point I've even forgotten the person's name. I could run into them tomorrow and not even link them to the event. Therefore, I harbour zero negative feelings about the person or the event. In fact, I'd not have remembered this story at all except for a moment a few weeks later in a Starbucks parking lot.

The morning light, the sour taste of the Starbucks new and "improved" matcha tea (a taste so bad it effectively broke a $200.00-per-month habit within about three weeks), combined for a moment for a recollection of that missed call—but still not the specific person.

After realizing that I had no negative feelings about this experience, I decided I'd try to get something positive out of it by sharing the story with you. Perhaps the next time you have a negative experience or emotion these steps will work for you:

Step 1: Immediately forgive, sincerely. (*You have no idea what is really going on in their life.*)

Step 2: Immediately reschedule a task that you know needs to be addressed. (You know you've a long to-do list.)

Step 3: Maximize your newfound time no matter where you are or how much time it is by being as productive as possible. Focus on getting positive things done. Don't waste your time by wasting someone else's time calling them to complain.

Step 4: Don't tell the story to anyone. Ever. Forget it and move on.

Telling the story won't make you feel better. In fact, it stands to make you feel worse; it will be like reliving the experience over and over again. That, in turn, will decrease your productivity. Don't dig that groove into your brain any deeper. Move forward into new positive stories and create a future of ***action***. There is little to be gained dwelling on the past.

It's crucial to step outside your own world for a moment in order to realize that virtually everyone around you is going, has gone, or is about to go through some sort of mid- to high-level trauma or has a friend or family member going through some sort of mid- to high-level trauma. People are all under pressure, not just you.

Fight the urge to complain. Fight it by doing. Doing what you can to make other people's lives easier and thus your own life that much more wonderful and productive!

CHAPTER 17

BRICK BY BRICK

"In the end, there can be only one."

—RAMIREZ

The word "priorities" rose from obscurity about 50 years ago, and by definition of the root word "priority" we are fooling ourselves to think that we can be focused on more than one important thing at a time. A true priority will consume 100% of our resources at any given time.

1. The quality of being earlier or coming first compared to another thing; the state of being prior.

In bankruptcy law, a business' debt to its employees has ***priority*** *over its debt to a landlord, so the employees must be paid first.*

When it comes to how you use your time, you are always paying somebody first. You can only make eye contact, or mental contact, and a genuine deep connection, with one person at a time. It's not something you can multi-task.

Be a single-tasker.

This is a book about managing relationships. Relationships with clients, referral partners, lenders, staff, and the world at large. Let's wrap this up on a deeper note; let's talk about something truly important; let's address the most important relationship you've got, not the one with your parents, your partner, or even your children. Ask any airline flight attendant and they will back me up on the suggestion that the most important relationship you have is the one with yourself—after all, in the event of an emergency, who do you place the oxygen mask on first?

If you do not take care of yourself first, you cannot take care of anyone else. Have I felt guilt for going to the gym at 6pm on my way home from work, or heading to a Bikram class at 10am on a Sunday morning, or just getting out for an hour's walk or a ride in the woods? Yes, I have. We all have so many other responsibilities to so many other people.

But if we do not stay fit & healthy, mentally fresh and sharp, then how will we serve these people? We will serve them poorly, they will get a subpar version of our "best."

Relationships are built much the same way anything worth building is, one building block at a time. A body is built one rep at a time, a brain is built one experience at a time, a career is built one deal, yes I said deal, at a time. It all begins with a foundation of constant space repetition.

Constant Spaced Repetition.

Don't skip reps, especially when it comes to building your foundation, because everything else in your life is supported by these four walls, the four walls of your foundation.

Brick by brick.

The four walls represent:

1. Spiritual/Mental Health
2. Physical Health
3. Social Relationships - Family & Friends
4. Business/Career Stability

Destruction

Any foundation can be destroyed by any number of forces.

Dynamite

Wrecking ball

Hurricane

Erosion

Random things do happen, accidents, health issues, divorce, etc., hitting one or more walls at the same time. How we react to them dictates the real outcome. Not the event itself.

Often these four walls are dismantled brick by brick by the very person who built them in the first place through long-term purposeful neglect. Think of the fifty-something high school ball player now carrying an extra hundred pounds, gained at a pace of just 3lbs per year.

In the past I've spoken about how each file you process is a brick in your foundation. With each successful file being the equivalent of a brick, and each failed file being the mortar that holds the bricks together.

Every single additional file that you choose to work after say 6pm is a brick in your business wall. But it's not a fresh brick, you've run out of those after 10–12 hrs in the office. No, it's almost certainly a brick stolen from another of life's foundations; personal relationships or personal health to name the two most vulnerable.

Before long your four walls may be looking like those of an old Western storefront. One wall painted brightly, rising up twenty or thirty feet like a manufactured peacock's tail saying "look at me." We see these people as the #1 salesperson, month after month, year after year, with a wall of awards, or as the ripped six-pack bodybuilder, or as the super-parent that shows up for every single school activity, field trip, and committee. But what do those other three walls look like?

In nearly every case, a peek behind the tallest wall will show us three others in need of love and attention.

Think on this.

A CHECKLIST

I wrote the following on a flight between Vancouver and Toronto in the summer of 2018, I handed it out to several dozen Mortgage Brokers at the workshop the next day, and more than a few have followed up saying that it really put some things in perspective for them. So I add it as one of my final thoughts for how you may want to approach your business, and your life.

My Opinion

I understand that my position is one where I lead by example at all times. *I must hold myself to a higher standard each and every day.* However, this does not make me "special." It just makes me "me."

If I'm going to advise my clients that they have certain things in place to better protect them and their families, then I too will have these things in place to protect myself and my own family.

I will not counsel on being INC, on having a current Will, on being insured for life, disability, or critical illness through MPP and/or an independent solution, unless I too have these things in place, or have at the very least gone through the application process.

Going through each process, having each of these things in place, *or being rejected*, will enable me to learn from the experience and to be better able to understand the stressors involved for those whom I advise. This, in turn, will make me a better advisor to my clients.

The Checklist

- ☐ Will(s)
- ☐ Incorporated
- ☐ Hold Co for investments
- ☐ Whole Life Insurance held in Corp
- ☐ Family Trust
- ☐ Quality Accountant
- ☐ Quality Bookkeeper synced with Accountant
- ☐ Certified Financial Planner (fee for service)
- ☐ Life Insurance 2M$ minimum (*no matter who you are*)
- ☐ Critical Illness 200K
- ☐ Disability – Long Term
- ☐ Disability – Short Term ***MPP***
- ☐ Annual Executive Physical

x____

Dated_______________

THE LAST WORD(S)

This book is meant to provide short, punchy thoughts on topical issues in business and in Brokering.

I hope the fire in your belly is burning and you are in high gear on the road to improving all aspects of your life, not just your business.

Problems are solved by thoughtful action. Inaction never got anyone anywhere. Be thoughtful, be nice, work hard, and maintain control.

Thank you.

ABOUT THE AUTHOR

As of 2019, Dustan Woodhouse is a three-time author and now the president of Mortgage Architects, a national team of more than 1,300 Mortgage Brokers across Canada with an aggregate production of $7 billion per year. In a field of 18,000 Canadian mortgage brokers, Dustan ranked "Top 20" for seven years running, with his personal production exceeding $100 million for three years running, winning "Broker of The Year" in 2017.